tacular growth of the S
t fleet, which doubled
from t' ft' scv

The Economics
of Soviet
Merchant–Shipping
Policy

The University of
North Carolina Press
Chapel Hill

The Economics of Soviet Merchant-Shipping Policy

by
Robert E. Athay

HE
847
.A85
1971

To my family

Preface

During the past decade the Soviet Union has assumed a major role in world ocean shipping. This development has produced concern and even anxiety in the Western world, particularly among individuals and groups involved in merchant shipping. The program to expand the Soviet merchant fleet has been widely discussed from the standpoint of its political and military implications, but it has received little attention from Western economists. This study was undertaken in the belief that Soviet behavior in the area of maritime affairs could best be understood if examined within the context of that country's over-all foreign economic policies. I have not intended this study as a comprehensive economic analysis of all aspects of Soviet merchant-shipping activities, but have restricted it mainly to an evaluation of the contribution of Soviet shipping policy to the country's broader economic objectives.

This book was made possible by the support of the Center for Naval Analyses, where I am employed, but the views expressed in it are my own and should not be attributed to my employers. I received helpful suggestions and criticisms from many individuals during the course of this study. Among these, W. Donald Bowles, Rush V. Greenslade, Warren S. Hunsberger, and Penelope H. Thunberg, all of whom helped guide the work from its inception, deserve special mention. All errors and omissions are, of course, my own responsibility.

Contents

Tables

The Economics
of Soviet
Merchant-Shipping
Policy

I

The Problem
and Methods
of Analysis

THE PROBLEM

The rapid expansion of the Soviet merchant fleet in recent years has given rise to considerable concern in the West regarding the motivations and goals of Soviet shipping policy. Western observers frequently have expressed the view that the build-up of the Soviet merchant fleet has been motivated largely by political and/or military considerations and have concluded, either explicitly or implicitly, that the Soviets have pursued this program with little concern for the economic costs involved. Soviet spokesmen have, of course, disclaimed any such intentions, stating that the expansion of their merchant fleet has been prompted by economic considerations, particularly by a desire to conserve foreign exchange.

Economic analysis cannot fully explain the motives and ultimate goals of Soviet shipping policy. It can, however, provide a useful check as to whether that policy has had a plausible economic rationale.

This study assesses the extent to which the heavy commitment of resources to the Soviet merchant fleet has been worthwhile from the standpoint of economic efficiency. The analysis involves a comparison of the real benefits obtained from ocean shipping to the real costs incurred, that is, the opportunities foregone in devoting resources to the program. In recent years the Soviets have become increasingly aware of the necessity of improving economic efficiency if satisfactory rates of economic growth are to be maintained. Numerous innovations in economic policy have been adopted to achieve that end.

METHODS, SCOPE, AND LIMITATIONS OF THE ANALYSIS

Economic activity in the Soviet Union is directed toward the attainment of goals determined by the central-planning authorities, that is, "planners' preference" has been substituted for "consumer preference." The professed goal of Soviet economic policy is to provide the highest possible level of consumer welfare, but this is to be achieved only when the millennial state of full communism has been reached. In the interim, the "building of communism" is to be facilitated by striving for high rates of economic growth, subject, of course, to constraints imposed by political considerations. The rate of economic growth is in large part a function of the efficiency with which resources are utilized, and the efficiency of an economic endeavor may be evaluated by comparisons of resource use in that activity with other Soviet industries and with similar activities in other countries. The allocation of resources to Soviet merchant shipping would be optimized at the point where the marginal returns to resources so committed were just equal to those from their most advantageous alternative uses and no incentive would exist for transferring resources between merchant shipping and other uses. This study does not attempt to show, however, whether or not the rate of Soviet investment in this industry has been "optimal," but only to show if such investments have involved a significant economic return.

In the Soviet economy prices and resource allocations are determined by the central-planning authorities, and the obstacles in the path of achieving an efficient allocation of resources are formidable.

First, Soviet concepts of cost accounting vary considerably from those employed in market economies. In the Marxist context, all values are derived from labor inputs; capital and materials contribute to the value of production only to the extent that they impart embodied labor. Thus, virtually the only capital charges employed are depreciation allowances, which are too small to have much influence on money costs.[1]

1. Capital charges in the Soviet Union do not reflect adequately either the time factor or relative scarcity. They consist essentially of depreciation allowances

Second, Soviet industrial prices—those that are applied to the transfer of goods within the state sector of the economy—often bear little or no relationship to either the scarcity of goods or to the demand for them, and furnish a poor basis for central planners to choose among alternatives concerning production and investment.

A third barrier to economic efficiency has arisen from ideological constraints that have prevented the adoption of objective economic criteria in allocating resources.

In spite of these deficiencies money costs are used in this study because they can be adjusted so that they are at least informative as measures of the real costs of resources used in ocean shipping. The greatest single weakness in Soviet cost data results from the absence of adequate capital charges. This has been corrected, at least crudely, by imputing interest charges. Soviet fuel prices include turnover taxes, which must be adjusted for on the basis of data for an earlier period. Soviet prices are even less meaningful in reflecting utility than in indicating cost; consequently, they could not be used to measure the real value of benefits. For this reason, and because the Soviets themselves have continually emphasized the importance of balance-of-payments criteria in shaping their merchant-shipping policy, the efficacy

---

(generally termed amortization charges in both the Soviet- and English-language literature), which do not represent prices for the use of capital assets as such, but charges for their consumption, with provisions for major repairs. Minor investments are sometimes financed with interest-bearing credits, but these are of minor significance.

Amortization charges in most industries represent a small share of total costs and moderate variations in these charges arising from changes in the rate of capital utilization do not alter total costs significantly. As a consequence, lower-level economic agencies and enterprises tend to select capital intensive variants from among possible resource combinations and project designs. They have no incentive to seek patterns and levels of capital utilization that are rational from the standpoint of the economy as a whole. They attempt, rather, to acquire as much capital as possible, since they regard it essentially as a free good, and because even excess capital assets are useful, among other things, as a hedge against uncertain production assignments in the future and for bargaining purposes for other items that may be required. These tendencies are abetted by the absence of penalties for accumulating superfluous assets. Amortization charges are not levied on uninstalled equipment.

Problems related to investment criteria and capital allocations are probably the most widely discussed aspect of the Soviet economy. Summaries of these problems are contained in Alec Nove, *The Soviet Economy: an Introduction* (rev. ed.; New York: Fredric A. Praeger, 1965), pp. 218–26; and George R. Feiwel, *The Soviet Quest for Economic Efficiency: Issues, Controversies, and Reforms* (New York: Fredric A. Praeger, 1967), pp. 113–19.

of investments in merchant shipping as a policy of import substitution has been adopted as the main measure of benefits.

ORGANIZATION OF THE STUDY

The remainder of the study consists of four substantive chapters, a summary chapter, and an epilogue. Chapter II sketches the development of the Soviet merchant fleet since the early 1950's and shows how changes in Soviet foreign trade have affected the Soviet demand for ocean shipping.

Chapter III is an evaluation of Soviet shipping costs. The major elements of cost are examined individually and their relationships to total costs are discussed. The influence on shipping costs of such factors as changes in the volume, direction, and composition of Soviet foreign trade, developments in the technology of shipping, and the Soviet institutional environment constitute important parts of this section.

Chapter IV assesses the benefits of Soviet merchant-shipping policy. The analysis in this chapter is largely in terms of the foreign exchange earned or saved. The ruble costs to the Soviets per dollar of foreign exchange saved by substituting domestic shipping services for foreign shipping are compared with ruble-dollar ratios calculated in a similar fashion for other items in the Soviet trade accounts. These comparisons provide an indication of the relative merits of Soviet investments in merchant shipping from the standpoint of improving the country's balance of payments and contributing to economic efficiency.

Ruble earnings from merchant shipping are shown in both Soviet accounting terms and adjusted terms. The resulting measures of "profitability" are meaningful in determining whether or not the industry has been self-sustaining in a budgetary sense—which sheds some light on its appeal to Soviet planners—as well as in real economic terms.

Soviet comparative advantage in merchant shipping is evaluated by comparing Soviet outlays for the major items of expenditure (capital, labor, and fuel) with those experienced by major ship operators in Western Europe and Japan. These comparisons shed light on the relative Soviet cost position and reveal areas of strength and weakness in the Soviet program.

The assessment of benefits also includes the consideration of a number of intangible factors, largely of a political nature.

Chapter V consists of an evaluation of the comparative efficiency of resource use in Soviet merchant shipping relative to other areas of the Soviet transport and communications sector and to Soviet industry. This analysis is meant to provide an alternative indication of the relative economic merits of investments in merchant shipping. It is recognized that the data are not ideal for such purposes but they are thought to be at least suggestive. These comparisons are based on data from Soviet literature on merchant-shipping operations and from various studies of factor productivity in the Soviet economy.

Chapter VI presents a summary of the analysis and a brief concluding statement. The epilogue discusses the present and prospective future impact of the Soviet merchant fleet on world shipping.

II

Development of
the Soviet
Merchant Fleet

*FOREIGN TRADE AND THE DEMAND FOR
OCEAN SHIPPING*

In the mid-1950's the Soviet Union increased both the intensity
and scope of its foreign economic activities. At the beginning of that
period Soviet foreign trade was both very small (2.9 billion rubles),
and highly concentrated with other communist countries (81 percent
by value).[1] Since most of those countries bordered the USSR, their
trade with the Soviets moved principally overland or by inland water-
ways. Thus, only a little more than a quarter of Soviet import and
export cargoes were sea-borne in 1950 (Table 1). The geographic
distribution of Soviet sea-borne trade also was very limited, 90 percent of it being with countries in continental Europe.[2]

Because of the low volume and narrow geographic distribution of
its sea-borne foreign trade, the USSR's demand for ocean-shipping
services in the early 1950's was small, and it was able to carry a

---

1. V. A. Kolesnikov and Ye. D. Rodin, "Osnovnyye osobennosti morskogo
transporta v sisteme yedinoy transportnoy seti SSSR" (Basic Peculiarities of
Maritime Transport in the Unified Transport System of the USSR), *Ekonomika
morskogo transporta morskoy transport v sisteme yedinoy transportnoy seti SSSR,
Trudy 6(12)* (Moscow: Transport, 1965), p. 13. Unless otherwise noted, 1961
rubles (1 ruble equals $1.10) are used throughout this book. Foreign-trade values
for the years prior to 1961 have been converted to 1961 rubles. Ruble prices used
are those in effect July 1, 1955.

2. *Ibid.*

TABLE 1. *Soviet Foreign Trade, Total and Sea-borne, Selected Years, 1950–1968*

(millions of tons)

	Total Trade	Sea-Borne Trade	Percent Sea-Borne	Carried in Soviet Ships	Percent in Soviet Ships
1950	30.2[a]	8.3[a]	27	5.9	72[b]
1958	69.6[c]	26.6[c]	38	14.6	55[b]
1959	85.6[d]	34.8[d]	41	16.4	47[e]
1960	99.3[d]	44.3[d]	45	18.2	41[e]
1962	132.9[d]	66.9[d]	50	24.8	37[b]
1965	173.9[f]	91.8[f]	53	46.4	50[g]
1967	206.7[h]	108.8[h]	53	56.6	52[i]
1968	217.8[h]	111.9[h]	51		

a. V. A. Kolesnikov and Ye. D. Rodin, "Osnovnyye osobennosti morskogo transporta v sisteme yedinoy transportnoy seti SSSR," in *Ekonomika morskogo transporta morskoy transport v sisteme transportnoy seti SSSR, Trudy 6(12)* (Moscow: Transport, 1967), p. 13.

b. *Ibid.*, p. 42.

c. *Ibid.*, p. 14.

d. Ministerstvo Vneshnei Torgovlii SSSR Planova-Ekonomicheskoye Upravleniye, *Vneshnyaya torgovlya soyuza SSR za 1959–1963 gody* (Moscow: Vneshtorgizdat, 1965), pp. 26–27.

e. *Byulleten tekhniko-ekonomicheskoy informatsii morskogo flota*, 11 (61) (Leningrad, 1962), p. 8.

f. *Vnesh., torg.* (1965), p. 20.

g. Soviet Embassy, Ottowa *Soviet News Bulletin*, May 16, 1966.

h. *Vnesh. torg.* (1968), p. 18.

i. V. G. Bakayev, *SSSR na mirovykh morskykh putyakh* (Moscow: Transport, 1969), p. 24.

substantial majority of that trade in its own ships (Table 1). In the mid- and late-1950's Soviet foreign trade increased rapidly. In 1958 the physical volume of Soviet foreign trade exceeded the 1950 volume by 130 percent (Table 1). Sea-borne trade increased even more rapidly, by 220 percent, and accounted for 38 percent of Soviet foreign-trade tonnage in 1958 as compared with 27 percent in 1950 (Table 1).

During this period an abrupt change occurred in the commodity structure of Soviet foreign trade as exports of petroleum and other bulk cargoes were greatly expanded. The share of Soviet sea-borne foreign-trade tonnage accounted for by exports increased from 44 percent in 1950 to 85 percent in 1958.[3] The expansion of Soviet

3. *Ibid.*, p. 5.

foreign trade also brought about changes in its geographic distribution. The relative importance of trade with other communist countries declined from 81 percent in 1950 to 74 percent (by value) in 1958.[4] Much of the increased trade with the non-Communist world was with the less developed countries of Africa, Asia, and Latin America. These countries' share of Soviet foreign trade increased from near negligible levels in 1950 to just over 10 percent (by value) in 1958.[5]

The trends in Soviet foreign trade that developed during the 1950–58 period continued during the next decade—but the rate of change was somewhat slower. The average annual rate of increase in the value of Soviet foreign trade declined from just over 14 percent in 1950–58 to 7.3 percent in 1959–68.[6] The rate of increase in the physical volume of Soviet sea-borne foreign trade also declined, but it grew by nearly 11 percent per year during 1959–68, which was considerably faster than the rate of growth in the value of trade, and in 1968 about 51 percent of Soviet import and export cargoes went by sea routes.[7] Exports commanded an ever-larger share of Soviet sea-borne trade tonnage, accounting for about 90 percent in 1968.[8] Trade with the Communist countries declined in relative importance to 67 percent of the total value of Soviet foreign trade in 1968, while trade with the industrialized West rose to 21 percent of the total and that with the less developed countries to 11 percent.[9]

EXPANSION OF THE SOVIET MERCHANT FLEET

To satisfy the growing demand for shipping services arising from the expansion and diversification of its foreign trade, the USSR could choose from among a limited range of alternatives. It could provide these services from its own resources, it could import them, or it could use a combination of imported and domestic shipping services. Like other trading nations, the USSR has combined imported

4. *Ibid.*, p. 13.
5. Ministerstvo Vneshnei Torgovlii SSSR Planova-Ekonomicheskoye Upravleniye, *Vneshnayaya torgovlya soyuza SSR za 1959–1963 gody* (Foreign Trade of the USSR in 1959–1963 (Moscow: Vneshtorgizdat, 1965), p. 11. Hereinafter referred to as *Vnesh. torg.* with appropriate year.
6. *Vnesh. torg.*, 1968, p. 8.
7. *Vnesh. torg.*, 1959–63, pp. 26–27, and *Vnesh. torg.*, 1968, p. 18.
8. *Vnesh. torg.*, 1968, p. 16.
9. *Ibid.*

shipping services with those provided by its own fleet. It has, however, sought to achieve a high degree of self-sufficiency in this field. Specifically, the Soviets have declared that they intend eventually (a) to carry all of their c.i.f. exports and f.o.b. imports in domestic bottoms,[10] and (b) to eliminate the loss of foreign exchange arising from chartering by increasing foreign-exchange earnings by Soviet ships to at least cover foreign-exchange expenditures for Soviet chartering of foreign ships.[11]

In pursuing this policy the USSR expanded its merchant fleet from approximately 2 million deadweight tons (dwt) in the early 1950's to about 12 million dwt at the end of 1968, when the Soviet fleet ranked as the sixth largest in the world.[12]

The Soviet fleet grew moderately during the last years of the Stalin regime, but the major emphasis on expansion came after 1953. At the end of World War II the Soviet fleet consisted largely of small coastal freighters and American lend-lease ships. Between 1946 and 1953 modest additions were made to the fleet and by the end of that period it approximated 2 million dwt. The rate of acquisitions accelerated after 1953. The new additions were obtained mostly from the communist countries of East Europe and Finland, as naval construction retained a high priority in Soviet yards during the early 1950's and imports from the West were inhibited by restrictions imposed on exports to the Soviet Union. In the five years between 1953 and 1958 the fleet tonnage was expanded by about 80 percent, to 3.6 million dwt.[13]

With the advent of the Seven-Year Plan (1959–65), the build-up of the Soviet merchant fleet entered a new phase. The relaxation of restrictions on exports to the USSR in 1958, and the generally

10. V. G. Bakayev, *Ekspluatatsiya morskogo flota* (Operation of the Maritime Fleet) (Moscow: Transport, 1965), p. 52. When goods are sold on a c.i.f. basis (cost, insurance, and freight), shipping charges are included in the selling price. When they are purchased f.o.b. (free on board), shipping charges are not included in the selling price and are provided at the buyer's expense.

11. *Vodnyy transport* (Water Transport), April 26, 1966.

12. United States Department of Commerce, Maritime Administration, *Merchant Fleets of the World* (Washington: United States Government Printing Office, 1969), pp. 6–7. Deadweight tonnage signifies the maximum carrying capacity of a ship expressed in tons of 2,240 pounds.

13. Committee on Commerce, United States Senate, *The Growing Strength of the Soviet Merchant Fleet* (Washington: United States Government Printing Office, 1964), p. 5.

depressed conditions in the ship-building industry of the West, led to a sharp increase in ship purchases by the Soviets from that area. Construction in domestic shipyards and imports from the Communist countries in Eastern Europe also were accelerated. A variety of ship types were added to the fleet during that period, including several series of general-purpose cargo vessels, ships with reinforced hulls for use in the heavy ice encountered on the Northern Sea Route, two new series of timber carriers, two series of small- to medium-sized bulk dry carriers, and several new series of tankers.

The new ships contributed significantly to the qualitative as well as the quantitative improvement of the Soviet merchant fleet, since they were generally larger, faster, and more efficient than ships acquired earlier. This is best illustrated by the improvements embodied in the new tanker series.

Before 1959 the Soviet tanker fleet consisted almost exclusively of ships in the Kazbek series, of which some seventy were built in the Soviet Union between 1951 and 1962. These were small, general-purpose tankers of 11,500 dwt, with a low maximum service speed of 13 knots. After 1959 the Soviets acquired several series of new and much larger tankers of both foreign and domestic construction. Among the first of these were the Pekin-class tankers built in Leningrad. These ships had a cargo capacity of 27,000 dwt and a service speed of about 18 knots. A follow-up series was built in the same yard beginning in 1962. Ships in this series—the Sofiya class—were of 45,000 dwt and the largest merchant ships built in the Soviet Union to the present time. Among the new tankers imported after 1959 were the Druzhba and Mir series of 35,000 and 36,000 dwt from Japan, the Trud series of 23,000 dwt from Yugoslavia, and the Adler and Gurzuf series of 23,000 dwt from Holland.[14]

Between 1963 and 1965 the USSR took delivery of two additional classes of tankers from Japan and Italy. These were the Lisichansk series of 32,000 dwt and the Leonardo da Vinchi class of 46,000 dwt. During this same period a number of smaller tankers were purchased by the Soviets from East European builders. The Bauska type of 16,000 dwt from Poland, the Split series of 18,000 dwt from Yugoslavia, and the Pevek class of about 4,000 dwt, designed largely for

14. A. L. Golovanov (ed.), *Transport SSSR itogi za pyatdesyat let i perspectivy razvitiya* (Transportation in the USSR, A Summary of Fifty Years and Perspectives for Development) (Moscow: Transport, 1967), p. 136.

the coastal trades and purchased from Finland, were among this group.[15]

During the first four years of the Seven-Year Plan (1959–62), the new tonnage added to the Soviet merchant fleet averaged about 600,000 dwt per year. The rate of growth quickened in the last three years of the plan period, when new acquisitions reached about 1 million tons per year. By the end of 1965 the Soviet fleet of ocean going merchant ships totalled about 8.5 million dwt.[16]

The 1966–70 plan called for the further expansion of the Soviet merchant fleet by about 50 percent, to approximately 13 million dwt. By the end of 1968 the Soviet fleet was estimated by the U.S. Maritime Administration to comprise 1,634 ocean-going steam and motor ships of 1,000 gross tons and larger, aggregating 11.9 million dwt. The composition of the Soviet fleet by vessel type was reported as follows:[17]

	Total	Freighters	Bulk Carriers	Tankers	Combination Pass.-cargo
Number	1,634	1,103	134	322	75
Tonnage (000's dwt)	11,911	6,564	752	4,398	198

Because of the rapid growth of the Soviet merchant fleet in recent years it is one of the "youngest" and most modern merchant fleets in the world. As of 1967 more than 80 percent of Soviet merchant ships were less than ten years old. Two-thirds of them have speeds in excess of 14 knots, and nearly all of them are powered by diesel or steam turbine engines.[18] The Soviets have lagged, however, in the development of container shipping and in acquiring large tankers and bulk carriers. The first container ships will not enter the Soviet fleet until the 1971–75 Five-Year Plan.[19] The largest tankers currently in the Soviet fleet are less than 50,000 dwt and the largest bulk carriers are 23,000 dwt, while tankers in excess of 300,000 dwt and bulk carriers

15. *Ibid.*

16. V. G. Bakayev, *SSSR na mirovykh morskykh putyakh* (The USSR on the World's Seaways) (Moscow: Transport, 1969), p. 21.

17. U.S. Maritime Administration, *Merchant Fleets of the World*, pp. 6–7. Gross tons denote the internal cubic capacity of a ship expressed in 100 cubic feet per ton.

18. Bakayev, *SSSR na mirovykh morskykh putyakh*, p. 2.

19. "Soviet Container Ships Set," *New York Times*, October 13, 1969.

of more than 100,000 dwt have become fairly common in the merchant fleets of Western countries. Notwithstanding the vast changes that have been made in the Soviet fleet in recent years, the average Soviet merchant ship is still smaller and slower than the average of the world's merchant fleet.

ADMINISTRATION

Merchant shipping in the USSR is a state monopoly conducted by the Ministry of the Maritime Fleet, which has jurisdiction over both the merchant fleet itself and a broad range of shore-based support installations, including ports, ship-repair yards, training facilities, and research and design institutions.

The ministry has fifteen regional-operating shipping lines (*paro-khodstva*) distributed among the five Soviet sea basins. Each shipping line is responsible for the ports and other shore facilities concerned with shipping operations within its prescribed area as well as for the ships assigned to it. A recent Soviet publication provides the following description of these shipping lines and their operations.[20]

Four shipping lines operate out of the Baltic Sea Basin. The largest of these is the Baltic Line based in Leningrad. This line operates largely general-cargo vessels and timber carriers engaged in foreign-trade shipping. It also runs a number of passenger lines.

The Latvian Line is based in Riga. It handles Soviet petroleum shipments in the Baltic Basin and operates a fleet of medium-tonnage dry-cargo and refrigerator ships.

Ships of the Estonian Line, which has its home port at Tallinn, carry dry cargoes in domestic commerce and also serve a number of European and West African ports. The Lithuanian Line, based in Klaipeda, began operations in January, 1969.

There are two shipping lines in the North Sea Basin. They are the Murmansk Line and the North Sea Line. The Murmansk Line operate: a large fleet of icebreakers serving the Northern Sea Route as well as dry-cargo vessels engaged in scheduled liner runs to Montreal. The North Sea Line operates from Arkangel'sk and is concerned largely with carrying exports of timber and wood products to a variety of foreign countries.

The five shipping lines serving the Black Sea–Azov Basin operate

20. Bakayev, *SSSR na mirovykh morskykh putyakh*, pp. 17–20.

more than half of the ships in the Soviet merchant fleet. The Black Sea Line (Odessa) has the largest fleet of dry-cargo ships in the country and operates world-wide. Ships of this line are engaged in regular liner service to India and Egypt, and in passenger service to many foreign countries.

The Azov Line, serving out of Zhdanov, specializes in the coal and ore trades. In addition to foreign-trade cargoes, this line carries nearly all of the domestic commerce in the Black Sea–Azov Basin.

The Novorossiysk Line operates the USSR's largest tanker fleet. It carries petroleum cargoes from the Black Sea–Azov region to ports in some fifty-five countries. The recently established Georgian Line (Batumi), operates a number of small- and medium-sized tankers on relatively short hauls to the Mediterranean and Red Seas and in domestic trade.

The Danube Line is occupied largely with Danube River shipments, but also carries trade between Izmail and Reni and ports in the Mediterranean and Red Seas.

Merchant shipments in the Soviet Far East are carried out by three shipping lines. The Far East Line, based in Vladivostok, operates dry-cargo ships, tankers, and passenger liners serving both Soviet and foreign ports. Much of the traffic of this line is over the Northern Sea Route.

The Sakhalin Line (Kholmsk) serves as the main transportation link with the Soviet mainland and carries timber and wood cargoes in foreign trade. The Kamchatka Line (Petropavlovsk–Kamchatka) serves a similar function for the Kamchatka Peninsula and carries timber and wood cargoes to Japan.

The single shipping line in the Caspian Sea Basin is the Caspian Line operating from Baku. This line serves Soviet ports in the Caspian and in recent years has carried foreign-trade shipments through the Volga–Don Canal and the Volga–Baltic Waterway.

A number of service and support organizations are directly subordinated to the Ministry of the Maritime Fleet. Prominent among these is "Sovfrakht," the agency having sole jurisdiction over chartering foreign tonnage to carry foreign-trade cargoes as required by the various Soviet foreign-trade organizations operating under the Ministry of Foreign Trade, and for chartering Soviet ships to carry cargoes for foreign shippers. Other organizations operating directly under the ministry include the Central Scientific-Research Institute of the Maritime Fleet in Leningrad, the Scientific-Research and Planning Design Institute in Moscow, two planning-design bureaus, one in Leningrad and the other in Rostov, and a number of higher and intermediate schools for training in the various maritime professions and trades.[21]

OPERATIONS

As indicated earlier, Soviet foreign trade began a sharp and persistent upswing in the 1950's, and sea-borne trade increased even more rapidly as a result of the diversification of Soviet trade with respect to its geographic distribution and its commodity structure. Expansion of the Soviet merchant fleet resulted in a rapid growth in the volume of shipments, and as Soviet trade became more widely diversified, the average length of haul became longer. Consequently, fleet performance, measured in ton-kilometers, rose more rapidly than the volume of cargo carried. Between 1950 and 1958, for example, the cargo tonnage carried by the Soviet merchant fleet increased from 34 million tons to 71 million tons, or by 108 percent, while fleet performance grew from 39 billion ton-kilometers to 106 billion ton-kilometers, or by 171 percent. The average length of haul increased from 1,178 kilometers to 1,502 kilometers during the same period.[22] Rapid rates of growth in both the volume of shipments and fleet performance continued throughout the decade following 1958. In 1968 the Soviet fleet carried 147 million tons of cargo and fleet performance reached 587 billion ton-kilometers, or 108 percent and 456 percent respectively, above the levels attained in 1958. The average length of haul in 1968 had increased to 4,000 kilometers.[23]

But even the rapid increase in Soviet merchant tonnage and the volume of cargo carried during the early and mid-1950's was insufficient to keep pace with the growth in Soviet sea-borne foreign trade, and the share of that trade the USSR was able to carry in its own ships declined sharply. In 1950 72 percent of Soviet sea-borne foreign trade

21. Golovanov, *Transport SSSR*, p. 128.
22. Tsentral'noye Statisticheskoye Upravleniye pri Sovete Ministrov SSSR, *Transport i svyaz' SSSR statisticheskii sbornik* (Transportation and Communications in the USSR a Statistical Compilation) (Moscow: Statistika, 1967), p. 151. Hereinafter referred to as *Transport i svyaz'*. Soviet shipping statistics are sometimes reported in miles and sometimes in kilometers. For purposes of consistency, kilometers are used throughout this study.
23. *Ekonomicheskaya gazeta* (Economic Gazette), No. 34, August, 1969, p. 7.

was carried in domestic bottoms; this share declined to 55 percent in 1958 and 37 percent in 1962 (Table 1). After 1962 the share of that trade carried in Soviet ships increased, reaching 52 percent in 1967.[24] Because of the continued rapid growth in Soviet sea-borne foreign trade during this period, however, the tonnage of Soviet foreign-trade cargoes carried in foreign-flag ships also increased.

Soviet merchant-shipping operations have become world-wide in scope. In 1967 Soviet ships visited 848 ports in 94 countries.[25] In spite of the growing geographic dispersion of Soviet shipping, however, it remains concentrated in a relatively few areas, as the following tabulation of visits by Soviet merchant ships to foreign ports in 1967 shows:[26]

	Port Calls	Port Visited
North, Central, and South America	2,333	95
Northern and Western Europe	7,269	330
Mediterranean, Black, and Red Seas	4,956	177
West Africa	479	26
Indian Ocean and East Africa	1,289	69
Southeast Asia, Oceania, and Australia	756	56
Japan, Korea, and Red China	1,892	95
Total	18,794	848

Nearly two-thirds (64 percent) of the total port calls by Soviet merchant ships in 1967 were in Northern and Western Europe, the Mediterranean, and the Black and Red Seas.

Most of the USSR's foreign trade is still with other Communist countries—67 percent by value in 1968—but much of that trade is not sea-borne, and consequently only about a quarter of the foreign-trade cargoes carried by the Soviet merchant fleet is in commerce with these countries. Shipments to and from the industrially developed countries of the West account for the largest share of the foreign-trade cargoes carried by the Soviet merchant fleet, but shipments between the Soviet Union and the less developed countries of the non-Communist world grew rapidly during the 1960's, as the following tabulation indicates:[27]

24. V. G. Bakayev, *SSSR na mirovykh morskykh putyakh* (Moscow: Transport, 1969), p. 24.
25. *Ibid.*
26. *Ibid.*
27. *Ibid.*

	1960		1967	
	Mil. Tons	Percent	Mil. Tons	Percent
Shipments between the USSR and:				
Communist countries	6.3	31.4	16.4	25.5
Developed Free-World countries	11.5	57.2	37.3	58.0
Less-developed Free-World countries	2.3	11.4	10.6	16.5
Total	20.1	100.0	64.3	100.0

As a means of increasing the foreign-exchange earnings of their merchant fleet, the Soviets have made determined efforts to increase the participation of their ships in the cross-trades, that is, in shipments between non-Soviet ports. The volume of cargo carried by Soviet ships in these trades increased from 1.9 million tons in 1962 to 15.7 million tons in 1967.[28]

The Soviets have expanded regularly scheduled liner service in order to make shipping in Soviet vessels more attractive to foreign-cargo owners. In 1967 more than thirty scheduled lines linked ports in the USSR with foreign ports.[29] Many of these lines were served jointly by Soviet and foreign ships.

28. *Ibid.*
29. Golovanov, *Transport SSSR*, p. 113.

III

Voyage Costs
of the Soviet
Merchant Fleet

This chapter examines and evaluates cost relationships in Soviet merchant shipping. The main discussion is preceded by a consideration of the nature of ocean-shipping costs and a description of the limitations that have been placed on the scope of the analysis.

THE NATURE OF OCEAN-SHIPPING COSTS AND THE SCOPE OF THE ANALYSIS

The total costs of ocean shipping may be represented as the aggregate of the following: vessel operating and maintenance costs; vessel capital charges; port dues and charges; and cargo handling expenses. This chapter is focused on the first three of these cost categories and the "shipping costs," as used herein, shall refer to voyage costs of merchant vessels, or those costs that are incurred dockside-to-dockside. Cargo handling expenses and general administrative costs will not be treated in detail because the appropriate data are not available.

The following expression identifies the major elements of shipping costs:

$$C = C_l + C_f + C_k + C_m + C_b,$$

where C_l = the cost of labor, including wages, social insurance deductions, and crew subsistence; C_f = the cost of fuel consumed; C_k = the cost of capital, determined by the original construction (or purchase) cost of the ship; C_m = the maintenance cost of the ship plus stores; and C_b = port dues and charges including port taxes, pilotage, dockage, sanitation, wharfage, anchorage, etc.

Total shipping costs are thus the sum of the component costs, which are determined by the unit prices of the various production factors, the physical properties of the ship, and the characteristics of the trade route. The relationship of total costs to the major cost elements and their determinants are examined below to show how changes in key variables influence total shipping costs.

The Relationship of Speed to Costs

The speed at which a ship is designed to travel is an important determinant of its operating cost. But when modern merchant ships are operating at or near their minimum-cost design speeds, fairly large changes in speed produce only minor changes in costs. Thus a curve showing total costs as a function of speed, with other parameters held constant, is dish-shaped.

The shape of the curve results from the decline in the number of days at sea necessary to complete a voyage as speed increases. The daily costs of ship operation increase with speed, but up to the point of minimum-cost speed the decline in the number of days at sea required to complete a voyage more than offsets the increase in daily operating costs. The reduction in the days at sea for a given voyage distance resulting from a given increase in speed is proportionally greater at low initial speeds than at high ones.

The ratio of distance to port time is important in determining the effects of speed on voyage costs. The greater the voyage distance with respect to port time, the greater "sea-costs" will be in relation to "port-costs," and the more critical speed will be in determining total costs.

Substitution between production factors can be accomplished through changes in design speed. Within certain limits, an increase in design speed results in a substitution of fuel for both capital and labor. In the low speed ranges, higher speeds mean lesser quantities of capital and labor per voyage. This follows even though daily consumption of these factors increases with speed.

An increase in ship size results in a much less than proportional increase in the minimum-cost speed and a decrease in the curvature of the total cost curve. The increased flatness of the cost curve means that the penalty for increasing the speed of a large ship beyond the optimum point is less than for a small ship. This accounts for the correlation between speed and size observable in modern merchant-ship design.

The Influence of Ship Size on Costs

The economies of scale in the design of merchant ships are well recognized. An increase in the size (cubic dimensions) of a ship leads to less than proportionate increases in costs. With other variables held constant, motive power and fuel requirements increase at about the same rate as ship size, but labor, capital, and maintenance costs increase less rapidly. Therefore, the cost per ton of capacity varies inversely with ship size.

To operate efficiently, however, high load-factors must be maintained. That is, the ship must be loaded as closely as possible to the practical limits of its capacity, since the costs of operating at less than capacity loads are approximately equal to those incurred when full loads are carried, and the revenues earned are commensurately less. The nature of the demand for the services of general-cargo vessels is such that in order to maintain suitable load-factors large vessels frequently must increase the number of ports of call, resulting in higher port-costs. This provides one of the major constraints on the optimum size of such ships. Port facilities and canals also place limits on ship size.

The constraints placed on the optimum size of general-cargo vessels by the nature of the demand for their services do not apply with equal force to bulk dry carriers and tankers, which can be operated on point-to-point runs at high load-factors in at least one direction. Moreover, the construction of off-shore facilities to load and discharge petroleum cargoes has made it possible to overcome the restrictions on tanker size imposed by the limitations of existing port facilities.

Voyage Costs as a Function of the Trade Route

The important variables in determining the costs of operating on a particular trade route are voyage distance, port time, and the number of ports of call. Since a proportionate increase in all of these variables leads to a proportionate increase in total voyage costs, the important considerations in guaging the effects of the variations in the trade route plied are the changes resulting from the relationships between these variables.

An increase in voyage distance, with other variables held constant, leads to a less-than-proportionate increase in costs and hence lower costs per ton-kilometer.

COST RELATIONSHIPS IN SOVIET OCEAN SHIPPING

The Soviet concept of production cost (*sebestoimost'*) has no equivalent in Western cost accounting. It includes direct and indirect labor costs, basic and auxiliary materials, amortization allowances, and overhead expenses. Land rent and interest charges on capital are omitted. As a result, the total costs are lower, and the relative costs are different from those that would be obtained if Western cost-accounting practices were used.

The "production" costs of ocean shipping include ship-operating costs but usually exclude stevedoring expenses and certain administrative charges incident to the management of shipping lines. Shipping costs are calculated on a ton-kilometer basis as follows:

$$C_{t-k} = \frac{E}{Q} = \frac{(a + b)tx + (a + p)tp}{Q},$$

where C_{t-k} = cost per ton-kilometer; E = the summation of voyage costs; Q = ton-kilometers of cargo carried on the voyages; tx = time in passage (in days); tp = time in port (in days); a = daily expenditures for ship operations (exclusive of fuel); b = daily expenditures of fuel in passage; and p = daily expenditures of fuel in port.

The structure of shipping costs incurred by the Soviet maritime fleet in 1958 and 1963 is shown in Table 2.

Expenditures for labor, fuel, and amortization are of approximately equal magnitude and together constitute about 70 percent of total shipping costs. The costs of current maintenance and repair—which are charged to operating costs—account for an additional 10 percent of the total.

Labor's share of total expenditures remained fairly stable from 1958 to 1963. The shares attributed to fuel and maintenance decreased during that period while the relative importance of amortization charges increased. The reduction in the share of total shipping costs attributable to fuel consumption arose largely from the acquisition of more efficient ships and the increase in average voyage distance. Lower maintenance and repair costs resulted from modernization of the fleet. Increased charges for amortization reflected shorter amortization periods as well as heavy capital expenditures in recent years.

The major components of Soviet shipping costs—capital, labor, and fuel—are discussed below to indicate the magnitude of the inputs of these factors to the shipping program and to shed some light on the comparative efficiency with which they have been utilized.

Capital

Ocean-shipping operations employ relatively large amounts of fixed capital; and capital charges account for a substantial portion of total shipping costs (see Table 2). As of January 1, 1964, the fixed capital of the Soviet Ministry of the Maritime Fleet (MMF) was divided as follows (in percent of total):[1]

Transport enterprises and organizations	91.1
Industrial enterprises (ship repair)	7.9
Other (construction, supply, and trade organizations, research, etc.)	1.0
	100.0

Merchant vessels accounted for 55.3 percent of the productive

TABLE 2. *The Structure of Soviet Ocean-Shipping Costs*[a]
(percent of total)

Item of Expenditure	1958	1963
Labor	26	25
Fuel	24	21
Amortization (including major overhaul)	19	24
Maintenance and repair	13	10
Supplies and stores	5	5
Port dues and navigation expenses	6	10
Administration and miscellaneous expenses	7	5

a. S. F. Koryakin and I. L. Bernshtein, *Ekonomika morskogo transporta* (2nd ed.; Moscow: Transport, 1964), p. 400.

1. S. F. Koryakin and I. L. Bernshtein, *Ekonomika morskogo transporta* (Economics of Maritime Transport) (2nd ed.; Moscow: Transport, 1964), p. 303.

fixed capital in transport enterprises and organizations and for about
50 percent of that of the MMF as a whole.[2]

Soviet acquisitions of merchant vessels during the period 1955–66
are shown in Table 3. Imports supplied about two-thirds of the
approximately 6.2 million deadweight tons (dwt) of shipping
acquired during that period. The largest share of the ships imported
came from other Communist countries, largely Poland and East
Germany. Japan, Italy, Denmark, Finland, and other Free-World
countries also were important suppliers.

TABLE 3. Deadweight Tonnage of Ships Constructed for USSR
Registry in USSR and Foreign Shipyards, 1950–1966[a]

(tonnage in thousands)

Year Built	Total	Comb. Passenger & Cargo	Freighters	Bulk Carriers	Tankers
1950	13		10	3	
1951	49	3	40	3	3
1952	76	3	39	15	19
1953	172		39	53	80
1954	281	1	95	55	130
1955	229	1	57	32	139
1956	345		106	95	144
1957	370		149	83	138
1958	229	1	114	64	50
1959	428	3	159	94	172
1960	636	11	188	149	288
1961	426	4	119	176	127
1962	740	4	240	191	305
1963	923	4	506	17	396
1964	1,100	12	411	32	645
1965	1,203	9	591	16	587
1966	1,027	9	536		482
Total	8,247	65	3,399	1,078	3,705

a. U.S. Department of Commerce, Maritime Administration, unpublished
tabulation of file data.

2. "Productive" capital, as defined by the Soviets, is that which contributes to
the production of material wealth, as distinct from "unproductive" capital such as
that in housing, recreation, and health facilities.

The heavy Soviet reliance on imported merchant vessels can be explained in the short run by the inability of domestic ship-yards to supply the tonnage required by the rapid expansion of the fleet. The continued dependence on imports as the major source of new acquisitions (about two-thirds in 1966) strongly suggests a competitive cost disadvantage in the Soviet ship-building industry vis-a-vis those of the countries from which Soviet imports come.

Data concerning the costs of ships imported by the Soviets are sketchy, but it appears that because of the highly competitive situation in the shipbuilding industries of the Free World, arising in large part from extensive idle capacity, the Soviets have been able to contract for ships on rather favorable terms. Moreover, imports from other Communist countries are believed to be based on world prices.

Although the Soviets have demonstrated a capacity to build a variety of merchant-vessel types and sizes, they have tended to concentrate on series construction of a relatively small number of designs. That production economies are derived from building a number of highly similar or identical ships is a favorite theme of Soviet discussions of shipping and ship building. The cost of the twelfth Kazbek-type tanker built, for example, was reported by one Soviet writer to have been only 55 percent of the cost of the first one.[3] Another Soviet author claimed more modest benefits from series construction, stating that Soviet experience indicated that in relation to the cost of the first ship in a series, cost savings of 6 to 8 percent were achieved for the second ship, 10.8 to 11.5 percent on the fifth ship, and 12.5 to 13.5 percent on the tenth one. Production beyond the tenth unit resulted in further, but smaller, savings.

In spite of the savings achieved by series construction, Soviet writers complain of continued high ship-building costs. For example, the passenger ships *Moldaviya* and *Svanetiya*, both built in 1960, were reported to have cost 4.15 million rubles and 3.82 million rubles, respectively, as opposed to a planned cost of 2.5 million rubles for ships of that type.[4]

The unrealistically low charges placed on capital in the Soviet Union lead to overbidding for investment resources. As a consequence,

3. V. P. Kolomoytsev, *The Cost of Maritime Shipping* (U.S. Department of Commerce, Joint Publications Research Service Translation 14,874, 12 August, 1962), p. 148.
4. Koryakin and Bernshtein, *Ekonomika morskogo transporta*, p. 333.

projects often cannot be completed in the time anticipated because the required inputs are not available.[5]

That the maritime industry has not escaped this phenomenon is illustrated by the frequent complaints voiced by Soviet writers concerning delays in both ship building and shore construction. S. M. Bayev, a Deputy Minister of the Maritime Fleet, in a discussion of this problem in *Morskoy flot* noted that:[6]

The principal defect in capital construction may be traced to spreading monetary, material, and technical resources among an unwarranted large number of projects under construction. Some managers of steamship companies, port terminals, plants, and other enterprises try to get as much money as possible for capital construction and initiate new construction without considering whether there are resources and possibilities for placing the units into operation in a short time. . . . The building of many projects takes a long time and does not ensure a proper return on capital investments and, moreover, in some cases the technology of the projects under construction becomes outdated by the time operations begin.

Of the total volume of construction scheduled for completion by the maritime industry in 1963, 37 percent was unfinished at the end of the year, including 29 percent in ship building and 61 percent in shore construction.[7] Soviet writers have been particularly critical of the failure of the industry to adapt modern construction techniques to ports and ship-repair facilities and to utilize new methods developed

---

5. The lack of adequate capital charges and penalties for accumulations of excess capital assets encourage Soviet economic organizations at the producing level to acquire as much of these assets as possible. To obtain new fixed capital Soviet enterprises require both the financial means and, for a wide variety of items, authorization to purchase the assets in question from the state supply organization. Financial resources for investment purposes are acquired largely through grants from the state budget. The key to obtaining budgeted investment funds is to have the project included in the economic plan. This is frequently achieved by substantially underestimating project costs, which leads to the initiation of more projects than can be completed with available resources in the plan period. Additional resources necessary for the completion of the projects are requested after they have been started, but since the budget reserves are not adequate for these purposes, the projects are generally not finished in the time originally anticipated. George R. Feiwel, *The Soviet Quest for Economic Efficiency: Issues, Controversies, and Reforms* (New York: Fredric A. Praeger, 1967), pp. 113–19.

6. S. M. Bayev, "Morskoy flot v chetvertii god semiletki" (The Maritime Fleet in the Fourth Year of the Seven-Year Plan) *Morskoy flot* (Maritime Fleet), XXII (January, 1962), pp. 1–2.

7. Koryakin and Bernshtein, *Ekonomika morskogo transporta*, p. 331.

abroad. For example, a Soviet delegation visiting West Germany found that the construction of berths in that country required only one-third to one-half as much time as in the Soviet Union.[8]

The magnitude of capital inputs in Soviet merchant shipping can be estimated from published data relating to capital investments and to changes in the value of capital stocks.

As indicated in Table 4, the volume of capital investment in the Soviet maritime industry increased by approximately four times in the decade after 1955 and by more than twelve times in the twenty years following World War II. In absolute terms, investment in the maritime industry expanded from about 455 million rubles in the five years from 1946–50, to 1.3 billion rubles in the 1956–60 period, and 5.5 billion rubles (planned) in 1966–70.

TABLE 4. Capital Investment in Soviet Maritime Transport, 1928–1963 and 1964–1970 (Plan)[a]

(in millions of current rubles)

Period	Total	Maritime Fleet	Shore Construction
1928–32	53.9		
1933–37	77.3	25.0	52.3
1938–42	98.2	40.4	57.8
1943–44	142.0	53.4	88.6
1946–50	455.5	199.2	256.3
1951–55	749.7	456.0	293.7
1956–58	669.0	444.1	224.9
1959–63	1,813.0	1,290.0	523.0
1959–65	3,263.0	2,284.1	978.9
1966–70 (plan)	5,547.1		1,223.5 (ports only)

a. S. F. Koryakin and I. L. Bernshtein, *Ekonomika morskogo transporta* (2nd ed.; Moscow: Transport, 1964), pp. 328–30. Capital investment increased by 2.5 times in 1959–65 as compared with 1952–58. Capital investment in 1951–58 was 1,418.7 million rubles. Investment in 1951 estimated at 15 percent of 1951–55 total or 113.5 million rubles; therefore, capital investment in 1952–58 was 1,418.7 million rubles minus 113.5 million rubles or 1,305.2 million rubles; 1959–65 = 2.5 × 1,305.2. The fleet was to account for 70 percent of total investment. Capital investment in 1966–70 is scheduled at 1.7 times 1959–65 for the maritime industry as a whole, and 2.5 times for port construction.

8. *Ibid.*, p. 332.

Table 5 shows Soviet capital investment in productive assets in all branches of transport (since nonproductive investments are excluded, the values for maritime transport are lower than those in Table 4). During the period shown, the share of total transport investment accounted for by maritime transport remained stable at around 10 to 12 percent. Investment in railroad and river transport declined in relative importance, while that in other modes of transport—largely air and automotive—increased sharply.

TABLE 5. *Capital Investment in Soviet Transport (Productive Assets), 1951–1965*[a]

(millions of rubles, 1955 prices)

	Total	Railroads	Maritime	River	Other
1951–55					
(annual avg.)	1,346	697	139	166	271
1956–60					
(annual avg.)	2,413	1,018	252	200	943
1961	3,395	1,249	310	222	1,614
1962	3,659	1,358	409	225	1,667
1963	3,914	1,460	469	223	1,762
1964	4,121	1,490	518	238	1,875
1965	4,345	1,529	549	229	2,038

a. Tsentral'noye Statisticheskoye Upravleniye pri Sovete Ministrov SSSR, *Transport i svyaz' SSSR statisticheskii sbornik* (Moscow: Statisticka, 1967), p. 42. Excludes investment in nonproductive assets.

Another measure of capital inputs to the Soviet maritime industry can be derived for the period 1955–66 from data concerning changes in the value of capital stocks (Table 6).

Capital charges are reflected in Soviet shipping costs in the form of amortization deductions calculated on the basis of the original cost of the ship (for ships built before 1959 the replacement cost in January 1, 1960, prices is used), its expected service life, and the anticipated costs of major overhaul and refitting during the service period. The amount of the annual deduction for amortization is calculated as follows:

$$A = \frac{C + R - S}{T},$$

where A = the annual sum of amortization deductions; C = the

TABLE 6. *Value of Productive Fixed Capital in Soviet Maritime Industry and in Transport Vessels, 1958–1966*

(average yearly values—millions of rubles)

	Productive Fixed Capital and Working Capital[a]	Productive Fixed Capital[b]	Productive Fixed Capital in Transport Vessels[d]
1958		1,513[c]	757
1959		1,761[c]	880
1960	2,060	2.008	1,004
1961	2,300	2,242	1,121
1962	2,640	2,574	1,267
1963	3,080	3,003	1,502
1964	3,430	3,344	1,672
1965	3,910	3,812	1,906
1966	4,390	4,280	2,140

a. Tsentral'noye Statisticheskoye Upravleniye pri Sovete Ministrov SSSR, *Transport i svyaz' SSSR statisticheskii sbornik* (Moscow: Statistika, 1967), p. 161.

b. S. F. Koryakin and I. L. Bernshtein, *Ekonomika morskogo transporta* (2nd ed.; Moscow: Transport, 1964), p. 301 shows working capital as 2.8 percent of total capital in the maritime industry and 2.5 percent of the total of productive fixed capital and working capital. Therefore, productive fixed capital (column 2) is calculated at 97.5 percent of productive fixed capital and working capital (column 1).

c. *Transport i svyaz' SSSR*, p. 39, indicates that the value of productive fixed capital in 1965 was 252 percent of that in 1958, 1959 interpolated.

d. Productive fixed capital in transport vessels accounts for about 50 percent of total productive fixed capital in maritime transport.

original (or replacement) cost of the vessel; R = the expected costs of repairs and refitting during the service life of the vessel; S = the estimated salvage value of the vessel at the end of its service life; and T = the service life of the vessel (in years).

The "norm" (rate) for amortization is expressed as the percentage relationship between the sum deducted annually for amortization and the original value of the merchant vessel:

$$N_a = \frac{A \times 100}{C}$$

The "norms" established by the Soviet government for amortization deductions have varied over time as have the proportions of total deductions allocated to capital repairs and to replacement. Before 1949 amortization deductions were not sufficient to cover capital repair costs, and, consequently, part of such costs and all expenditures for new investment in the maritime fleet were financed by allocations from the state budget. Beginning in 1950, amortization deductions were designed to cover all capital repair costs and from 1951 a small portion of the new investment expenditures as well.

Until about 1960, the service life of Soviet merchant vessels was determined solely by physical wear; obsolescence ("moral wear" in Marxist terminology) was of little or no significance. Merchant vessels were kept in service for long periods by means of extensive repairs that in some cases resulted in expenditures as much as 100 percent in excess of those required to construct new ships of comparable size.[9] That the amortization charges for the replacement of capital in the Soviet maritime fleet were not sufficient for the purpose is borne out by the fact that the implicit service periods for merchant vessels in the mid- and late 1950's (based on then-current amortization norms) ranged from 80 to 116 years.[10]

The Soviet government adopted new amortization procedures for the maritime fleet following the capital census that was conducted throughout the economy in 1959. The new program was announced in 1961 and became effective January 1, 1963. Annual amortization deductions under the new procedures were increased significantly, reflecting much shorter service periods for merchant vessels. Obsolescence gained recognition as a factor determining the length of economically useful service.[11] A major weakness of the old amortization system was eliminated by valuing ships built before 1959 at their replacement costs in January 1, 1960, prices rather than at the

9. L. S. Turetskiy and O. A. Novikov, *Amortizatsiya osnovnykh fondov morskogo flota* (Amortization of Fixed Capital in the Maritime Fleet) (Moscow: Transport, 1963), p. 66.

10. *Ibid.*, p. 33.

11. Marx recognized that fixed capital could lose its economic value independently from physical wear, i.e., that it could become obsolete. He distinguished two types of obsolescence: (a) that which resulted from increased productivity (and lower costs) in the capital goods industries; and (b) that which arose from technological advances and permitted the use of more productive capital assets. The Soviets, however, long regarded obsolescence as a phenomenon arising from the profit motive and hence peculiar to the capitalist system. This interpretation has given way in recent years to the explicit recognition of obsolescence as a factor in capital costs. For example, the amortization procedures adopted in 1961 not only called for much shorter replacement periods for merchant vessels, but also provided for the creation of special funds for their periodic modernization. Koryakin and Bernshtein, *Ekonomika morskogo transporta*, pp. 309–11.

original cost. Ships added to the fleet since that time are carried at their original cost.

The norms established for the amortization of merchant vessels (in percent of original vessel cost) and the years of service life on which these norms were based, were as follows:[12]

	Total	Capital Repairs	Replace-ment	Service Life
Passenger and passenger-cargo vessels	5.9	2.6	3.3	30
Dry-cargo vessels	6.4	2.6	3.8	26
Tankers	7.8	3.3	4.5	22

The extent to which the service lives of Soviet merchant vessels were reduced by the new amortization norms is illustrated by the following tabulation showing the ages (in years) of the vessels retired during the Seven-Year Plan (1959-65):[13]

	Average	Minimum	Maximum
Passenger and passenger-cargo vessels	45	29	82
Dry-cargo vessels	39	15	70
Tankers	38	22	68

Labor

The manpower requirements of the Soviet merchant fleet have expanded greatly in recent years, some 80 percent of the current tonnage of the fleet having been added in the past decade. Employment in ships' crews totaled 25,300 in 1950; it increased to 47,900 in 1960, and to 67,200 in 1965.[14] Wage costs account for about 20 percent of total costs of Soviet ocean shipping; and indirect labor costs, which consist largely of expenditures for berthing and subsistence, and social insurance deductions, add an additional 5 percent.[15]

12. Charges for major overhaul and refitting vary with the type of ship and the kind of propulsion machinery used; the figures shown for capital repairs include a .5 percent charge for "modernization." *Ibid.*, p. 312.

13. Turetskiy and Novikov, *Amortizatsiya*, p. 68.

14. Tsentral'noye Statisticheskoye Upravleniye pri Sovete Ministrov SSSR, *Narodnoye khozyaistvo SSSR v 1965 godu* (The National Economy of the USSR in 1965) (Moscow: Statistika, 1966), p. 478. Hereinafter referred to as *Nar. khoz.* with reference to the appropriate year.

15. E. Korsakov, "The System of Remuneration in the Soviet Merchant Marine," *International Labor Review*, XCIV (October, 1966), p. 399.

The fleet is manned exclusively by Soviet nationals who are recruited and trained in establishments maintained by the Ministry of the Maritime Fleet. Soviet training of personnel for the merchant fleet is noteworthy in that it is concerned with providing not only ships' officers but also other licensed personnel and unlicensed seamen. The institutes also provide training for a wide variety of shore-based positions in the maritime industry.[16]

The allocation of a basic production resource in the Soviet Union through the operation of the price mechanism is unique to the labor market. Administrative controls over labor allocations are limited, for the most part, to the higher-skill categories. Graduates of higher training schools and technical institutes are obligated to serve where they are directed for stipulated periods, usually three to four years. Members of the Communist party and, to a certain extent, members of the Young Communist League (*Komsomols*) also are subject to such controls. Together these groups comprise a sizable portion of the technical and managerial personnel, but the bulk of the labor force, particularly those in the lower-skill categories, are free to change jobs in response to higher wages or other material incentives.

The wage system, based on the principle of pay in accordance with the "quantity and quality of work," features sharply differentiated rates between skill levels and the broad use of piece rates. To attract labor to preferred geographic areas or occupations, wage supplements based on the "conditions of work" are employed.

The Soviets rely largely on material incentives to attract the desired labor force to the maritime industry. A career in the merchant marine offers certain attractions that are generally not available to Soviet workers, such as the opportunity to travel (and purchase goods) abroad. Nevertheless, relatively high money wages provide the basic inducement to such employment.

The wage system used in the merchant fleet follows that of other nonagricultural sectors of the Soviet economy rather closely. It is founded on basic pay rates for each position plus various supplements, including bonuses for fulfilling and overfulfilling certain goals of the

16. Koryakin and Bernshtein, *Ekonomika morskogo transporta*, p. 357 reports the distribution of the labor force in the maritime industry as follows: ships' crews, 25 percent (67,200); port workers, 31 percent (83,300); ship repairs, 16 percent (43,000); other, including dredging, navigation aids, scientific research, and training institutes, 28 percent (75,000). Thus, total employment in the industry in 1965 was about 268,000.

monthly and annual plans, and regional differentials based on the vessel's port of registration.

Basic pay rates for officers are established in accordance with the individual's function, the size of the ship, and the power of the propulsion machinery and auxiliary equipment. For the purpose of determining pay scales for deck and engine-room officers, for example, vessels are divided into seven classes depending on their gross registered tonnage and the installed capacity of their main engines; for electrical officers, ships are divided into six groups in accordance with the aggregate power (in kilowatts) of the vessel's general electrical equipment; and for radio officers there are four groups of ships, depending on the character of the radio equipment carried.[17]

Since the degree of skill and responsibility required of individual nonrated crew members does not necessarily vary with the size of the ship or the power of its equipment, pay scales for these positions are structured solely on the basis of position. Larger vessels and those with more powerful equipment carry greater numbers of personnel in the higher-skill categories.

Wage scales are differentiated by geographic area as well as by skill level. The regional differentials are designed to compensate for higher expenditures for clothing, heating, etc., in the northern regions and for generally higher living costs in the northern and far eastern regions of the USSR. Differentials range from 1.2 to 1.8 times the rate paid for service on vessels registered in Black Sea ports. The highest differentials are paid for ships registered in Petropavlovsk or Kamchatka. Differentials are also paid for passages through areas of the Arctic, Antarctic, and tropics.[18]

Soviet merchant seamen receive supplements to their basic wages to compensate for hazardous or unpleasant conditions of work. For example, crew members on vessels carrying explosive cargoes or hot agglomerate are paid a 25 percent supplement to their basic wage, and those on vessels transporting petroleum products with a flash point below 28 degrees centigrade, such as gasoline and crude oil, are paid 15 percent extra from the time the vessel is loaded until it is unloaded and degassed.[19]

In order to provide greater incentives for efficient operation of the

17. Korsakov, "System of Remuneration," pp. 401–8.
18. *Ibid.*
19. *Ibid.*

merchant fleet, crewmen are paid bonuses when their ship meets or surpasses certain goals set by the periodic economic plans.[20] For ships engaged in transporting foreign-trade cargoes, bonus payments are determined by the relationship between expenditures in domestic currency and net foreign exchange earnings. In addition, crew mem-

TABLE 7. *Typical Remuneration of Officers and Men on a Kazbek-Type Tanker Navigating in the Black Sea Before and After the 1960 Wage Reform*[a]

Function	Old System (rubles per month)				New System (rubles per month)			Increase in earnings	
	Basic Rate	Bonus for 5% Overfulfillment of Voyage Targets and Monthly Plan	Seniority Supplement	Total	Basic Rate	Bonus for 5% Overfulfillment of Monthly Plan	Total	In Rubles	Percentage
Master	154.00	63.0	34.0	251.00	253.0	63	316.0	65.00	25.8
Second mate	93.25	38.0	19.0	150.25	159.5	40	199.5	49.25	32.7
Fourth mate	69.50	28.5	7.0	105.00	132.0	23	155.0	50.00	47.6
Chief engineer	143.00	58.5	34.0	235.50	231.0	58	289.0	53.50	22.6
Second engineer	96.25	39.5	26.5	162.25	187.0	47	234.0	71.75	43.2
Fourth engineer	77.75	32.0	11.0	120.75	126.5	32	158.5	37.75	31.4
Boatswain	59.50	18.0	17.0	94.50	115.5	29	144.5	50.00	53.0
Donkeyman	66.75	27.0	14.0	107.75	104.5	26	130.5	22.75	21.5
Deck rating class I	48.50	14.5	5.0	68.00	82.5	21	103.5	35.50	52.2
Deck rating class II	43.00	13.0	4.0	60.00	71.5	18	89.5	29.50	49.5
Motorman class I	55.65	16.7	7.0	79.35	88.0	22	110.0	30.65	37.8
Motorman class II	48.50	14.5	5.0	68.00	77.0	19	96.0	28.00	41.2

a. E. Korsakov, "The System of Remuneration in the Soviet Merchant Marine," *The International Labor Review*, XCIV (October, 1966), p. 410. Calculations are for an oil tanker of 8,300 gross registered tons, powered by two internal combustion engines with an aggregate of 5,000 horsepower.

20. The bonus system and its effects on the efficiency of the Soviet merchant fleet are discussed in more detail below.

bers directly engaged in tending fuel-consuming machinery are eligible for bonuses based on fuel economies achieved. The bonus scales are such that payments for meeting or exceeding one or more of the major plan goals comprise a significant share of the total money income of merchant seamen (see Tables 7 and 8).

TABLE 8. Typical Remuneration of Officers and Men on an Aleksander Suvorov–Type Cargo Steamer Navigating in the Black Sea Before and After the 1960 Wage Reform[a]

Function	Old System (rubles per month)				New System (rubles per month)			Increase in Earnings	
	Basic Rate	Bonus for 5% Overfulfillment of Voyage Targets and Monthly Plan	Seniority Supplement	Total	Basic Rate	Bonus for 5% Overfulfillment of Monthly Plan	Total	In Rubles	Percentage
Master	140.0	52.5	34.0	226.5	230	57.50	287.50	61.00	26.9
Second mate	85.5	32.0	17.0	134.5	145	36.25	181.25	46.75	34.7
Fourth mate	64.0	24.0	6.5	94.5	100	25.00	125.00	30.50	32.2
Chief engineer	130.0	48.7	34.0	212.7	195	48.70	243.70	31.00	14.5
Second engineer	95.5	35.8	25.5	156.8	160	40.00	200.00	43.20	27.5
Fourth engineer	71.5	26.8	10.5	108.8	105	26.00	131.00	22.20	20.4
Boatswain	55.0	20.0	11.0	86.0	100	25.00	125.00	39.00	45.4
Deck rating class I	45.0	13.5	4.5	63.0	75	18.80	93.80	30.80	48.8
Deck rating class II	41.0	12.3	4.0	57.3	65	16.20	81.20	23.90	41.8
Machinist class I	47.5	14.2	6.0	67.7	80	20.00	100.00	32.30	47.7
Machinist class II	42.5	12.7	5.0	60.2	70	17.50	87.50	27.30	45.4

a. E. Korsakov, "The System of Remuneration in the Soviet Merchant Marine," *The International Labor Review*, XCIV (October, 1966), p. 412. Calculations are for a Liberty-type vessel of 8,000 gross registered tons powered by a main engine of 2,500 horsepower.

The current wage system in the maritime industry became effective in 1960 as part of a comprehensive revision of wages throughout the Soviet economy. The previous system was introduced in 1946, and because of changes in the merchant fleet since that time it had become badly outdated. The 1960 wage reform resulted in wage increases averaging approximately 30 percent, but were generally much higher for the lower pay grades.[21] The wage reform was accompanied by a reduction in the work day from eight to seven hours for most merchant seamen. The reduction in the number of hours worked per shift increased manning requirements by approximately 7 percent and gave additional impetus to mechanization and automation.[22]

The money wages of Soviet merchant seamen were reported to have averaged 1,550 rubles annually (or 129 rubles per month) "in recent years" by a 1965 Soviet source.[23] This figure compares rather closely with average monthly wages of 128, to 134 rubles for all workers and employees in Soviet water transport for the years 1963–65 as reported in an official statistical publication of the Soviet government.[24]

The number of crew members required to man a ship depends largely on the type and size of the ship, the type and capacity of the power plant and auxiliary equipment, and the degree of automation and mechanization. An increase in the physical dimensions of a ship, by itself, results in a much less than proportionate increase in crew requirements; generally, only the number of seamen need be increased. The type, capacity, and complexity of the ‚power plant and auxiliary equipment, on the other hand, are critical determinants of crew size. Motorships and liquid-fueled steamers require fewer firemen, for example, than do steamers operating on solid fuels. The addition of refrigeration equipment or complex electrical systems increases the need for maintenance personnel.

The crew sizes of Soviet merchant ships of standard design are established by directives of the Ministry of the Maritime Fleet. The manning scales currently in effect were set in April, 1963.[25] Crew

21. Korsakov, "System of Remuneration," p. 408.
22. N. I. Povalyayev, "Ekonomicheskiye pokazateli vos 'mi i semichasovogo vakht i sudovykh rabot" (Economic Indexes of Eight-Hour and Seven-Hour Shifts in Shipboard Labor), in *Voprosy ekspluatatsiya morskogo transporta Trudy* 7(*13*) (Operating Problems in Maritime Transport) (Moscow: Transport, 1965), p. 72. A survey of 402 Soviet merchant ships before and after the shift to a seven-hour working day showed an average increase in crew size of 7.3 percent.
23. *Ibid.*, p. 80.
24. *Nar. khoz.*, p. 567. The average monthly wage in water transport was 134.0 rubles in 1965—the highest reported for any sector of the Soviet economy. The average monthly wage for the economy as a whole in 1965 was 95.6 rubles; for production workers in industry it was 103.3 rubles; and for workers in science and science services (the second-highest category) it was 115.6 rubles.
25. Koryakin and Bernshtein, *Ekonomika morskogo transporta*, p. 387.

sizes for nonstandardized ships are determined by the individual steamship lines on the basis of established standards.

The crew complements of Soviet merchant ships increased somewhat during the early 1960's. One Soviet author claimed that in 1957 crew sizes were some 20 to 25 percent larger than in 1935.[26] The tables of organization of ships' crews were revised in 1957 and some redundant positions were eliminated. Additional reductions were made possible through the practice of "mixing professions," which allowed crewmen to be trained to perform more than one function. Thus a fireman could be trained to fill in as deckhand when needed. As a result of these and other measures crew sizes reportedly were cut by 3 to 5 percent between 1961–62 and 1964.[27]

The current crew sizes for a number of Soviet freighters are shown in Table 9.

TABLE 9. Crew Sizes of Soviet Freighters[a]

Name of Ship	Cargo Capacity (thous. tons)	No. in Crew
Tissa	1.0	28
Pervomaysk	2.5	39
Donbass	4.0	43
Vil'nyus	5.8	43
Chelyuskinets	6.7	41
Belorussiya	7.0	46
Leningrad	9.0	40
Volgales'	5.0	38
Dzhankoy	8.6	39
Leninskiy Komsomol	13.0	57

a. Ya. B. Kantorovich, *Ekonomika morskogo sudna* (Moscow: Transport, 1964), p. 76.

It is apparent from the table that manpower requirements are much lower in proportion to cargo capacity on the larger ships. Moreover, since the larger ships also tend to be faster (for reasons explained earlier), their efficiency is further increased.

26. Ya. B. Kantorovich, *Ekonomika morskogo sudna* (Economics of the Maritime Ship) (Moscow: Transport, 1964), p. 71.
27. *Ibid.*, p. 72. The adoption of the seven-hour working day has tended to offset such gains.

The Seven-Year Plan (1959–65) called for an increase in labor productivity in merchant shipping of 45 percent, of which 13 percent was to result from increased cargo capacity of the fleet; 25 percent from more modern ships, higher speeds, and more time underway relative to time in port; 2 percent from lower organization tables for crews; and 5 percent from labor savings arising from "mixing professions."[28] The Seven-Year Plan goals were reached before the end of 1963 (according to Soviet data) and were surpassed by a considerable margin by the end of 1965, the last year for which data are available (Table 10).

TABLE 10. *Comparative Growth of Labor Productivity and Average Wages in Soviet Merchant Shipping, 1953, 1958, 1960, and 1963–1965*

	Output per Worker		Average wage	
	Ton-Km. per Man-Year[a]	Index (1953=100)	Rubles per Month[b]	Index (1953=100)
1953	1,571	100	93.2	100
1958	2,420	154	97.9	105
1960	2,774	177	106.0	114
1963	3,981	253	128.3	138
1964	4,719	300	131.6	141
1965	5,801	369	134.0	144

a. Tsentral'noye Statisticheskoye Upravleniye pri Sovete Ministrov SSSR, *Transport i svyaz' SSSR statisticheskii sbornik* (Moscow: Statistika, 1967), p. 159.
b. Tsentral'noye Statisticheskoye Upravleniye pri Sovete Ministrov SSSR, *Narodnoye khozyaistvo SSSR v 1965 godu* (Moscow: Statistika, 1966), p. 567 is the source for the years shown from 1958–65. Ya. B. Kantorovich, *Ekonomika morskogo sudna* (Moscow: Transport, 1964), p. 70 states that average wages in merchant shipping increased by 5 percent from 1953 to 1958.

The increase in labor productivity in Soviet merchant shipping (as measured by ton-kilometers of cargo performed per worker) apparently outstripped the increase in average wages by a considerable margin during the period 1958–65, indicating a sharp decrease in unit labor costs.

Fuel

Outlays for fuel account for slightly more than 20 percent of the total operating expenses of the Soviet merchant fleet. This share

28. Koryakin and Bernshtein, *Ekonomika morskogo transporta*, p. 386.

has remained fairly constant, but there are considerable variations between ship types and trade routes.

Calculations based on 1959 data show that for the Soviet merchant fleet as a whole, variations in fuel consumption between ships with different power plants were as follows, in kilograms per 1,000 tonnage-miles:[29] for the relatively few steamships still operating on solid fuel, 53.5; for steamships operating on liquid fuel, 34.9; and for motorships, 11.0.[30]

The change in the composition of the Soviet merchant fleet in favor of ship types that are more economical in terms of fuel consumption is shown in Table 11.

TABLE 11. Soviet Merchant Ships by Engine Type[a]

(percent of total fleet tonnage)

	1939	*1958*	*1963*
Steam piston engines (including combined installations)	69.1	46.4	32.0
Turbines (including turbo-electric)		4.1	11.0
Diesel (including diesel-electric)	30.9	49.5	48.1

a. S. F. Koryakin and I. L. Bernshtein, *Ekonomika morskogo transporta* (2nd ed.; Moscow: Transport, 1964), p. 175.

The acquisition of ships with steam piston engines has been discontinued. The new ships added to the Soviet merchant fleet in recent years for the most part have been equipped with diesel and steam turbine engines. A relatively small number of ships with gas turbine engines has been acquired.

The 1960 prices of different types of liquid fuels in the USSR are shown in Table 12. They include the refinery price, shipping and storage charges, and turnover taxes. A zone pricing system is used for calculating shipping charges, and the country is divided into five

29. Tonnage-miles (a standard Soviet index of operating efficiency) is obtained by dividing the ton-miles of cargo actually performed by the percentage of utilization of the ship's full capacity. Thus ton-miles and tonnage-miles would be equal if capacity is fully utilized, but tonnage-miles exceed ton-miles at less than full capacity.

30. Kolomoytsey, *Cost of Maritime Shipping*, p. 155.

zones for this purpose. Maritime ports are located in three of these five zones. Zone I takes in the ports on the Black Sea and the Sea of Azov, Zone III covers the Baltic ports and Murmansk, and Zone V takes in the ports of the far eastern regions.

TABLE 12. *Prices of Liquid Fuels and Lubricants in the USSR by Zone, 1960*[a]

(rubles per ton)

	Zone I	Zone III	Zone V
Motor fuel	26	31	40
Diesel fuel	29–31	32–34	42–44
Mazut, furnace (sulphurous)[b]	18	23	32
Mazut, furnace (low sulphur)[b]	24.5	29	38
Mazut, fleet[b]	25	29.5	39
Motor oil	51	62	38
Cylinder oil	51	64	79
Turbine oil	78	93	77

a. V. P. Kolomoytsev, *The Cost of Merchant Shipping* (U.S. department of Commerce, Joint Publications Research Service Translation 14,874, 12 August, 1962), p. 130.
b. Soviet grades of black oil.

Petroleum depots are located in many of the larger ports; bunkering charges, therefore, are generally not large. In the ports of Baku and Batumi, for example, ships are bunkered directly from the moorage of the petroleum depot. In the Black Sea area as a whole, bunkering charges are equal to about 10 percent of the price of fuel.[31] Bunkering charges are higher in other areas, however. In the port of Leningrad, for example, ships are bunkered from a floating base, and bunkering and storage costs amount to 12 to 15 percent of the price of fuel. In Murmansk these charges amount to 30 to 38 percent of the selling price of fuel.[32]

The distribution of freight turnover between Soviet sea basins is shown in Table 13. As the table indicates, the areas with the greatest concentration of shipping are also the areas with lower fuel costs. Hence, the average costs of fuel are close to the lowest cost.

31. Kantorovich, *Ekonomika morskogo sudna*, p. 90.
32. Kolomoytsev, *Cost of Maritime Shipping*, p. 130.

TABLE 13. *Distribution by Sea Basin of Foreign-Trade Cargoes Handled by Soviet Seaports, 1962*[a]

(percent of total)

	Exports	Imports
Black Sea–Azov	63.2	59.6
Baltic	24.6	34.1
Northern	6.6	2.8
Far Eastern	5.4	9.8
Caspian	0.2	0.7

a. S. F. Koryakin and I. L. Bernshtein, *Ekonomika morskogo transporta* (2nd ed.; Moscow: Transport, 1964), p. 132.

Maintenance and Other Costs

Expenditures for maintenance and repair (excluding those for major overhaul and refitting, which are charged to capital expenditures) account for about 10 percent of the operating costs of the Soviet merchant fleet. In 1951 these charges accounted for 18 percent, and in 1958 for 13 percent of operating costs.[33] The decline in the relative importance of repair and maintenance expenditures has resulted largely from the reduction in the average age of ships in the fleet. But Soviet efforts to increase the efficiency of ship-repair operations has probably contributed significantly to this trend.

Because of the individual nature of ship-repair work, standardized norms and repair charges cannot easily be applied. Soviet repair yards, which have operated on a cost-plus basis, have apparently been rather inefficient. Not only have repairs been costly in monetary terms, but they also have been slow, thus reducing the ship's operating time and detracting from the over-all efficiency of merchant fleet operations.[34]

Soviet efforts to reduce repair costs and the time ships are laid up for repairs have included a number of schemes to provide greater incentive for efficient operations of ship-repair yards, increased mechanization of repair work, stricter regimes for preventative maintenance, and the utilization of crew members for repair work

33. Koryakin and Bernshtein, *Ekonomika morskogo transporta*, p. 446.
34. Kolomoystev, *Cost of Maritime Shipping*, pp. 175–83.

wherever feasible. Although these measures have apparently been at least partially successful, frequent comments in the Soviet trade literature testify to the continued high costs and delays encountered in ship-repair work.

Other Factors Influencing Shipping Costs

The Size and Speed of Ships. / The size of merchant ships and the speed with which they travel are important determinants of the costs of ocean shipping. An increase in ship size, with other variables held constant, results in lower capital and operating costs per ton of capacity. Economies often result from increased speed, particularly in the operation of larger ships. The mutual relationship of size and speed to cost has produced a world-wide trend toward both larger and faster merchant ships.

The development of the Soviet merchant fleet has followed precisely the pattern suggested by these two key determinants of efficiency. The average size of ships in the Soviet merchant fleet has increased several times since the end of World War II.[35] The dry-cargo ships acquired in 1965, for example, were approximately five times as large, on the average, as those acquired in 1950. The increase in tanker size has been equally pronounced.

The average service speed of ships in the Soviet merchant fleet also has increased sharply. The older and smaller tankers of the Kazbek type have a service speed of 12 to 13 knots, whereas those of the Warsaw and Sofiya classes have speeds of 17 to 18.5 knots. The service speed of lumber carriers of pre-World War II construction was 7 to 8 knots, but that of the newer models has been increased to 13 to 13.5 knots. The largest and fastest dry-cargo vessels currently in the Soviet fleet—those of the Leninskii Komsomol class— have service speeds of 18 to 19 knots.

The relationship between ship size and shipping costs in the Soviet merchant fleet is illustrated in Tables 14 and 15. Table 14 shows capital and operating costs of Soviet motor ships of varying size traveling at the same speed and over the same trade route. Unit

35. It should be noted, however, that as of the end of 1965 the average ship in the Soviet merchant fleet was still both smaller and slower than the average ship in the merchant fleets of the major maritime countries. U.S. Department of Commerce, Maritime Administration, *The Soviet Merchant Marine* (Washington: United States Government Printing Office, 1967), p. 32.

costs—for both capital and operating items—are clearly a declining function of ship size. Table 15 illustrates the reductions in shipping costs associated with the use of larger tankers on the Black Sea–Far East run in 1961. Here again, unit costs, expressed in rubles per thousand ton-kilometers, decline as ship size increases.

TABLE 14. Capital and Operating Costs of Soviet Freighters of Various Sizes[a]

	Ship Size (dwt)		
	3,000	5,000	10,000
Cost of hull (rubles/dwt)	650	500	475
Cost of power plant (rubles/ton)	1,650	1,500	1,450
Fuel costs (rubles/1,000 ton-km.)	.67	.53	.43
Crew (number)	38	46	52
Labor cost (rubles/1,000 ton-km.)	.46	.27	.19
Administrative and other indirect costs (rubles/1,000 ton-km.)	.23	.12	.09

a. S. F. Koryakin and I. L. Bernshtein, *Ekonomika morskogo transporta* (2nd ed.; Moscow: Transport, 1964), p. 161.

TABLE 15. Comparative Costs of Operating Tankers of Various Sizes, Black Sea–Far East Run[a]

(1961 data)

	Unit of Measure	Tanker Type		
		Kazbek	Warsaw	Sofiya
Size	dwt	11,585	30,000	47,750
Rated speed	knots	13.2	18.2	17.5
Length of run	miles	10,500	10,500	10,500
Carrying capacity of ship	mil. ton-km.	828	3,222	4,445
Investment costs per 1,000 ton.km.	rubles	4.2	2.0	1.8
Productivity of crew per man-year	mil. ton-km.	18.89	53.7	68.9
Shipping costs per 1,000 ton-km.	rubles	.57	.43	.35

a. S. F. Koryakin and I. L. Bernshtein, *Ekonomika morskogo transporta* (2nd ed.; Moscow: Transport, 1964), p. 164.

Table 16 shows how the average service speed of Soviet merchant vessels increased from 1940 to 1963. Table 17 illustrates the effects on costs, both total and by major item of expenditure, of varying the operating speed of a Soviet motor freighter of 13,000 dwt on a voyage of 10,000 miles (18,520 kilometers). The optimum speed for this vessel operating under the conditions stipulated is seen to be 15 knots. As speed is increased from 13 to 15 knots, the ton-kilometer costs of all items of expenditure except fuel decline, resulting in an over-all reduction in total costs per ton-kilometer. At speeds above 15 knots, expenditures for amortization and repair as well as those for fuel increase. The combined increase in expenditures for these items is sufficient to more than offset reduced expenditures for labor and other items, and total costs per ton-kilometer increase.

TABLE 16. Increase in Average Service Speed of Soviet Merchant Ships, 1940–1963[a]

(in percent)

	Dry-Cargo Ships	Tankers
1940	100	100
1950	107	101
1958	137	128
1963	165	160

a. S. F. Koryakin and I. L. Bernshtein, *Ekonomika morskogo transporta* (2nd ed.; Moscow: Transport, 1964), p. 170.

TABLE 17. Operating Expenditures of Soviet Motor Vessel as a Function of Speed[a]

(rubles per 10,000 ton-kilometers)

Speed (Knots)	Labor Costs	Fuel Costs	Amortization Repair and Supply Costs	Other Costs Including Navigation	Total Costs
13	.62	1.28	3.02	.44	5.36
15	.57	1.46	2.88	.40	5.31
17	.55	2.03	3.00	.38	5.96
20	.52	3.33	3.41	.35	7.61

a. S. F. Koryakin and I. L. Bernshtein, *Ekonomika morskogo transporta* (2nd ed.; Moscow: Transport, 1964), p. 173.

Volume, Direction, and Structure of Soviet Foreign Trade. |
Changes in Soviet foreign trade during the past decade have had
pronounced effects on the operating efficiency of the Soviet merchant
fleet. The sharp increase in the volume of foreign trade, the longer
voyage distances which arose from this expanded trade, and the shift
in the commodity composition of trade all contributed to reducing
the costs per ton-kilometer of cargo performed.

The sea-borne foreign trade of the Soviet Union has increased
sharply in recent years. In 1960 it totaled approximately 45 million
tons; during the next five years it more than doubled, reaching 92
million tons in 1965.[36]

The increased volume of freight traffic has contributed to the improved operating efficiency of the merchant fleet in a number of ways.
First, it is axiomatic in merchant shipping, as in other capital intensive
industries with high fixed charges, that higher operating levels lead
to lower average costs by spreading fixed costs over a large number
of units of output. Second, increased cargo flows have made the use of
larger ships more feasible and have enhanced the efficiency of support
operations.

As indicated earlier, there are significant economies derived from
the use of large ships, provided they can be operated at high load-
factors.[37] When cargo flows are light, it may be found that in order
to maintain an adequate load-factor for a large ship it is necessary to
increase the number of ports visited on a voyage. Additional port
calls generally add to total port time and hence to operating costs.

The larger volume of freight traffic has made possible the expansion
of the number and importance of regular cargo routes. This has helped
to lower shipping costs by cutting port time and improving cargo
handling and storage.[38]

An increase in voyage distance, other variables remaining constant,
results in a less than proportional increase in total voyage costs and
lower costs per ton-kilometer. This relationship can be illustrated as
follows:

$$C_{t-k} = \frac{P_{c-t}}{D_k} + S_{t-k},$$

36. *Vnesh. torg.*, 1965, p. 20.
37. The load-factor is the ratio of cargo carried to the usable cargo capacity.
38. Kolomoytsev, *Cost of Maritime Shipping*, p. 383.

where C_{t-k} = total voyage costs per ton-kilometer; P_{c-t} = port costs per ton; D_k = voyage distance in kilometers; and S_{t-k} = sea costs per ton-kilometer.

The ratio of port costs to voyage distance P_{c-t}/D_k governs the extent to which a change in voyage distance affects the costs of shipping per ton-kilometer. The larger D_k is in relation to P_{c-t} the more costs will decline as voyage distance increases.

The increase in the average length of haul by the Soviet merchant fleet for selected years from 1950 to 1965 is shown in Table 18. Although it is not possible to compare closely these changes with changes in port costs, it seems clear that the operating efficiency of Soviet ports has improved and that the increase in voyage distance (as shown in the table) has contributed significantly to lower ton-kilometer costs of sea-borne cargo movements.

TABLE 18. *Average Length of Haul by the Soviet Merchant Fleet, 1950–1965*[a]

(kilometers)

	Dry-Cargo Ships	Tankers
1950	669	1,896
1952	676	1,654
1953	650	1,685
1955	1,222	1,698
1959	1,676	2,046
1962	2,408	2,561
1965	3,821	3,661

a. Ya. B. Kantorovich, *Ekonomika morskogo sudna* (Moscow: Transport, 1964), p. 16. Includes coastal shipping. The average length of haul of foreign shipments in 1965 was 4,554 kilometers for the dry-cargo fleet and 5,549 kilometers for the tanker fleet.

Changes in Soviet foreign trade have influenced the operation of the Soviet merchant fleet not only through the increased volume of cargo and the longer voyage distances, but also through changes in the commodity structure of the cargo carried.

As pointed out in Chapter II, the rapid increase in Soviet foreign trade that began in the 1950's was accompanied by a shift in its commodity structure resulting from the sharp growth in exports of petroleum and other bulk items. The share of total cargo carried by the Soviet merchant fleet accounted for by petroleum rose from approximately 31 percent in 1950 to 52 percent in 1956.[39] In 1950, exports accounted for 43 percent of the tonnage of Soviet sea-borne foreign-trade cargoes, and in 1958 for 90 percent.[40]

The type of cargo carried has a significant effect on shipping costs. This arises from the facility with which the cargo can be handled in loading and unloading operations and the relationship between cargo volume and weight, which determines the degree to which the effective carrying capacity of the ship can be utilized. Liquid cargo (and bulk dry cargoes such as grain, coal, and metallic ores) can be loaded nearer to the ship's full carrying capacity than can general cargoes made up of units of unequal size and density. On the other hand, tankers and bulk dry carriers generally are able to secure cargo for only one direction on a voyage. Tankers are sometimes employed to carry grain or other dry cargoes on return voyages, but more often they are compelled to travel in ballast, which reduces the over-all utilization rates of such ships. Nevertheless, petroleum and bulk dry cargoes can still be shipped at lower unit costs than general cargo.

Institutional Factors. | Although innovations that have been made regarding the size and speed of ships employed in the Soviet merchant fleet and changes in Soviet foreign trade have been conducive to improved operating efficiency of the fleet, other forces have been at work that have tended to dampen that trend.

Soviet managerial practices have given rise to a variety of problems that bear on the efficiency of merchant-shipping operations. Management-associated problems are endemic in the Soviet system and of fundamental importance in the analysis of Soviet economic institutions, but this discussion must be limited to a cursory treatment of some of the more salient difficulties they have produced.

One such problem—and one that has proved to be a major impediment to efficiency throughout the Soviet economy—has arisen from the necessity of devising a system (or systems) of material rewards that would provide the kinds of incentives required to stimulate individual and group efforts toward the ends stipulated in the economic plan. Historically, the basic approach in Soviet industry has been to

39. *Transport i svyaz'*, pp. 153–54.
40. *Vnesh. torg.*, 1968, p. 18.

stimulate such effort by tying money income to the achievement or surpassing of established norms or "success indicators."

In the past, these systems were generally designed to maximize physical output, which frequently was pursued with little regard for efficiency, and which led to a whole series of new difficulties such as distortions in the product-mix, low-quality goods, and a reluctance to disrupt established procedures by adopting new technology.

The difficulties experienced with the incentive system in the merchant fleet are typical of those encountered elsewhere in the Soviet economy. Up to 1960 bonus payments in the merchant fleet were determined on the basis of the fulfillment or overfulfillment of plan goals expressed in terms of the physical volume of cargo carried, that is, in tons and ton-kilometers. The influence of this system on shipping operations was described by V. G. Bakaev, Minister of the Maritime Fleet, in 1965 as follows:[41]

> The plan, the wage system, and bonuses were the reasons why they were interested in as many tons and ton-miles as possible. It was of little concern to them whether it was profitable or not for the government and the Merchant Marine. Their desire to accomplish the index, more tons and ton-miles, and to avoid such freight as plywood, cotton, rubber, textiles, paper and other so-called cubic capacity (also one of the plan indexes) and which they considered as less profitable although this actually brought one and a half or twice as much income; to carry this freight, foreign ships were chartered at high foreign-currency rates.

In an attempt to provide stronger incentives for efficiency, a new bonus system was introduced in 1960 as part of the wage reform. This system ties bonus payments for the officers and crews of ships engaged in foreign voyages to the ratio of expenditures in domestic currency to net foreign-exchange income.[42]

41. *Izvestiya*, October 10, 1965, p. 2.
42. This ratio is expressed in index form by Koryakin and Bernshtein, *Ekonomika morskogo transporta*, p. 419 as follows:

$$I = \frac{\sum \overline{E}_R}{\sum \overline{T}_R},$$

where $\sum E_R$ = net expenditure—in ruble terms; $\sum \overline{T}_R$ = net foreign-exchange income—in ruble terms

$$\sum \overline{E}_R = E_R - (E\$ \cdot a);$$

where: E_R = ruble expenditure; $E\$$ = foreign-exchange expenditure; a = ruble

Other steps taken to improve the operating efficiency of the merchant fleet included expanding the authority of individual steamship lines to make decisions of local concern. The role of the ministry was to be limited to broader problems relating to technical developments and over-all planning. Although spokesmen for the ministry have credited these measures with a good deal of success, complaints continue to appear in the trade press concerning the stultifying effects of "petty-tutorship" and "arbitrary directives" from the central authorities.[43]

Errors in the central planning of cargo traffic have also given rise to complaints in the trade press from those on the operating level. One such correspondent questioned the wisdom of shipping pig iron to Japan from ports in the southern regions of the USSR when such shipments could be directed through northern ports and over the northern route to the Orient at a saving of some 10,000 miles. He charged that this problem occurred simply because the ministry did not devote sufficient attention to selecting optimum routes.[44]

The Ministry of the Merchant Fleet has resorted to electronic computers to aid in the solution of problems related to the efficient scheduling and distribution of cargo traffic and the proper assignment of vessels. An experimental computer center was established in Leningrad early in 1966 to serve the Baltic fleet. The center was to make recommendations for proper balancing of cargo flows through various ports, for determining the routes to which cargoes should be assigned in order to minimize shipping costs, and for coordinating vessel assignments with cargo routings in such a way as to minimize delays and ballast runs.[45] According to to a Soviet press release in December, 1966, the ministry was in the process of establishing a computer center in Moscow to resolve economic problems associated with sea-transport operations and to appraise conditions in world freight markets.

---

exchange rate—$\sum \overline{Y}_R = (Y\$ \cdot a) - (E\$ \cdot a)$; and where $Y\$ =$ gross foreign-exchange income.

For meeting the norms established for net foreign-exchange earnings for a merchant ship, all crew members receive a bonus of 15 percent of their base wage or salary; additional bonuses of 2 percent are paid for each percent overfulfillment of the plan goal, and 5 percent for completing the voyage on schedule.

43. *Vodnyy transport,* October 12, 1965, p. 1.
44. *Ibid.*
45. *Leningradskaya pravda* (Leningrad Pravda), January 18, 1966.

Summary of Voyage Costs in Soviet Ocean Shipping

Table 19 shows the average costs per ton-kilometer and estimated total expenditures for all Soviet merchant shipments for 1950, 1958, and 1960–66. The average cost of shipments per ton-kilometer declined by 38 percent from 1950 to 1958 and by an additional 37 percent from 1958 to 1966, for an over-all drop of 61 percent for the 1950–66 period.[46]

TABLE 19. *Total Expenditures in Soviet Merchant Shipping, 1950, 1958, and 1960–1966*[a]

(all voyages)

	Total Shipments (bil. ton-km.)	Unit Cost (kopeks/10 ton-km.)	Total Expenditures[b] (mil. rubles)
1950	40.7	3.74	152.2
1958	107.8	2.32	250.1
1960	133.3	2.12	282.6
1961	161.1	2.06	331.9
1962	175.4	2.00	340.8
1963	228.7	1.90	434.5
1964	300.4	1.67	501.7
1965	392.1	1.48	580.3
1966	446.1	1.46	651.3

a. Tsentral'noye Statisticheskoye Upravleniye pri Sovete Ministrov SSSR, *Transport i svyaz' SSSR statisticheskii sbornik* (Moscow: Statistika, 1967), p. 151 and p. 160. Shipments include passenger traffic at the rate of 1 passenger kilometer equals 1 ton-kilometer.

b. Column 1 times column 2. Total expenditures for merchant shipping are given in the source cited in footnote [a] for 1958, 1960, and 1964–66. They differ slightly (generally by less than 1 percent) from those shown here, which were calculated from total shipments and costs per ton-kilometer of shipments.

The Soviets have attributed these cost reductions primarily to the factors discussed above, i.e., larger, faster, and more efficient ships, an increased volume of foreign trade, and longer voyage distances.[47] The 1966–70 economic plan calls for further reductions in shipping costs of 17 percent for the dry-cargo fleet and 20 percent for the tanker fleet.[48]

46. Only minor price changes occurred during this period. Wages increased somewhat, but prices of fuel and other inputs to merchant shipping trended downward, or remained stable, especially after 1955.

47. *Vodnyy transport*, February 29, 1964, pp. 2–3.

48. "Novaya pyatiletka-zhivoy delo millionov" (The New Five-Year Plan— A Vital Concern of Millions), *Morksoy flot*, XXVI (January, 1966), pp. 1–3.

FREIGHT CHARGES IN SOVIET OCEAN SHIPPING[49]

Foreign-trade shipments account for by far the largest share of the ton-mile performance of the Soviet merchant fleet. Rate schedules for these cargoes are established by the Bureau of Prices of the State Planning Commission (Gosplan) on the basis of rates prevailing in international shipping markets. Freight charges for tramp shipments are based on charter market rates and liner rates are established for each line and commodity shipped. Rates on lines served jointly by Soviet and foreign ships are established by agreement and apply equally to all ships regardless of flag. On Soviet-operated lines the rates generally are competitive with—or lower than—those charged by foreign ships serving the same general areas.

In order that changes in world charter market rates may be reflected in rates charged by the Soviet merchant fleet, the Ministry of Foreign Trade and the Ministry of the Maritime Fleet may petition Gosplan for rate changes, but not more often than once each year. This is usually done in the period preceding the establishment of the annual economic plan.

Freight charges for foreign-trade cargoes are differentiated by product, with ten rate classes for dry cargoes, not including lumber and wood. Charges for carrying liquid cargoes are based on the rate for heavy petroleum products. The rate for light petroleum products, for example, is 15 percent higher than the basic rate, and for such products as alcohol, methane, and turpentine it is 25 percent higher.

Freight charges by the Soviet merchant fleet include stevedoring costs in foreign ports. That is, rates are quoted free-in for exports and free-out for imports.

Freight charges for shipping goods between Soviet seaports are largely cost-determined, as are other prices governing transactions between enterprises in the state sector of the Soviet economy. The guiding principle is that rates should be high enough to cover shipping costs and provide a small margin for profit. The value of the product shipped has a direct bearing on freight charges for only a small minority of items, such as high-value metals.

Different rate schedules are used for shipments within each of the five Soviet sea basins. Charges for shipments between sea basins are

49. Koryakin and Bernshtein, *Ekonomika morskogo transporta*, pp. 150–63.

based on a single schedule. All rate schedules are differentiated between dry cargoes and petroleum shipments.

Rate schedules consist of two parts; one based on costs experienced in the ports of origin and destination (port rates), and the other on costs incurred while the ship is underway (voyage rates). For purposes of calculating voyage rates, dry cargoes are divided into ten classes according to cubic volume per ton. The lower rates apply to high-bulk cargoes and the higher rates to products with high weight-to-volume ratios. Additional charges are levied for items that exceed established limits for size and weight, or that require refrigeration. Shipments on the Northern Sea Route also bear higher rates. Uniform voyage rates apply to all types of petroleum cargoes.

Port rates—for both dry cargoes and petroleum—are based on cargo handling costs, which may vary both with respect to the type of cargo and the port. There are seven classes of dry cargo used in calculating cargo handling rates, for example, and different rate schedules are used in each of the five Soviet sea basins. In the Black Sea–Azov region and in the Baltic uniform rate schedules apply to all ports, while in the remaining sea basins rates vary among ports in accordance with differences in their cargo handling costs.

IV

Benefits of Soviet Merchant-Shipping Policy

This chapter measures the benefits accruing to the Soviet Union from its merchant-shipping program. The analysis is focused on economic gains, but certain effects of a noneconomic nature also are considered.

Cost-benefit evaluations of alternative investment programs commonly are cast in terms of the net value of the anticipated cash flows arising during each year of the projects' lives discounted, at an appropriate rate, to a common base year. The project yielding the greatest margin of net benefits—other things being equal—is considered to be superior. Although cash flows are most frequently selected as the appropriate index of benefits, they are not always suitable for this purpose, since other effects of the investment program may take precedence over earnings, or because benefits may not be measurable in monetary terms.

It was pointed out in Chapter I that Soviet prices are poor indicators of scarcity values and that the monetary returns from economic activities do not, by themselves, provide an adequate measure of real economic benefits. For this reason, and because the Soviets have placed great emphasis on balance-of-payments problems in determining shipping policy, the effectiveness of the shipping program as a policy of import substitution has been selected as the chief measure of the economic benefits derived.[1] The effectiveness of the program

1. See, for example, the statement by V. G. Bakayev, Minister of the Maritime Fleet, in *Krasnaya zvezda* (Red Star), March 13, 1966, p. 1. It is recognized that

is judged in terms of its impact on the Soviet balance of payments and by comparing the results achieved with the probable results of certain alternatives.

THE SOVIET BALANCE-OF-PAYMENTS PROBLEM

The Soviet Union has experienced a chronic imbalance in its trade account with the developed countries of the Free World in recent years. This deficit was greatly increased in 1963–65 by the heavy imports of grain made necessary by short-falls in Soviet production.

Only fragmentary data are available relative to the nontrade components of the Soviet balance of payments, but it is apparent that a sizable deficit exists in capital transactions with the non-Communist world. Loans and credits extended to the less developed countries of the Free World (averaging $350–400 million in recent years) and Soviet repayment of Western credits have exceeded new credits drawn by the Soviets and repayments of loans by the less-developed countries.[2]

There is probably a small deficit with the Free World in invisible transactions because net Soviet receipts from tourism do not fully offset the net Soviet deficit in transportation expenditures. Transfer payments—chiefly Soviet military and economic grants, and payments to the U.N.—also produce a moderate deficit.[3]

The Soviet Union experienced deficits in its trade accounts with the hard-currency countries in each of the nine years from 1959 through 1967.[4] The cumulative Soviet deficit in hard-currency trade for this nine-year period was in excess of $2 billion. The Soviets cleared these

the Soviets have had much greater problems in settling their financial obligations with hard-currency areas than with countries with which they have been able to arrange clearing accounts, and that these problems have exerted a proportionately large influence on merchant-shipping policy. An attempt has been made, therefore, to estimate the impact of the merchant fleet on hard-currency balances and soft-currency balances separately.

2. Hertha W. Heiss, "The Soviet Union in the World Economy," *New Directions in the Soviet Economy*, Studies Prepared for the Joint Economic Committee of the United States Congress (Washington: U.S. Government Printing Office, 1966), Part IV, p. 932.

3. *Ibid.*

4. Joint Economic Committee, Congress of the United States, *Soviet Economic Performance: 1966–67* (Washington: United States Government Printing Office, 1968), p. 98.

deficits by selling gold in Western markets. The significance to the USSR of gold sales of such magnitude is indicated by the fact that Soviet gold reserves were estimated by an agency of the U.S. Government at "less than $2 billion" at the beginning of 1964.[5]

A significant part of Soviet imports from the industrial West consist of capital equipment and advanced technology not readily available to the Soviets from other sources. These imports enable the USSR to forego the expenditures of physical resources and time that would be required to develop them domestically. They are, therefore, an important element in Soviet economic planning and will likely remain so for as long as the USSR can so profit by this exchange.

Numerous aspects of Soviet trade practices in recent years reveal anxiety on the part of Soviet planners concerning problems in financing imports from hard-currency areas of the Free-World. Efforts to conclude bilateral arrangements whereby Soviet imports from Western countries are tied to Soviet exports to the same countries, Soviet attempts to finance imports through long-term credits, and requests for improved customs treatment of Soviet goods all suggest careful husbanding of foreign exchange and concerted endeavours to protect gold reserves.

Soviet ability to increase earnings of hard currencies through expanded exports to the West is limited. The USSR has, on occasion (and with some success), sought entry to world export markets by selling at substantially below existing market prices. Although the motives for these actions may have been mixed, it seems probable that the desire to gain hard-currency exchange was an important factor.

THE EFFECTS OF SHIPPING POLICY ON THE SOVIET BALANCE OF PAYMENTS

A Methodology for Measuring the Net Effects of a National Merchant Fleet on the Balance of Payments

Ocean freight charges constitute a significant share of the delivered (c.i.f.) prices of commodities traded in international commerce. Because expenditures for this purpose frequently are important

---

5. Legislative Reference Service of the Library of Congress, *A Background Study of East-West Trade*, Prepared for the Committee on Foreign Relations, Congress of the United States (Washington: U.S. Government Printing Office, 1965), p. 22. The Central Intelligence Agency is cited as the source of this estimate.

items in a country's balance of payments, the substituting of domestic ships for foreign ships in carrying the country's export and import cargoes seems to offer an attractive means of improving the country's foreign-exchange position. Additional revenues earned by the fleet in cross-trades, i.e., shipments that do not involve domestic ports, are viewed as net additions to the foreign-exchange balance. Upon closer examination, however, serious flaws appear in these contentions.

The impact on the balance of payments of substituting domestic for foreign ships cannot be measured by the foreign-exchange earnings of the domestic fleet, because this ignores the necessary foreign-exchange expenditures incurred in operating domestic ships in foreign areas. The net foreign-exchange earnings of the fleet in excess of foreign-exchange expenditures are still an inadequate test, since they do not take into account foreign-exchange revenues lost as a result of the reduced sale of goods and services to the foreign vessels replaced by the domestic fleet. The relevant measure of impact is the net difference in the country's balance of payments from what it would have been if the substitution of domestic ships for foreign ships had not taken place.

A methodology has been developed by R. O. Goss[6] that permits the net difference in the balance of payments resulting from the expanded use of domestic ships where foreign ships were formerly used to be isolated by adjusting the foreign exchange earned thereby for increased spending arising from operations in foreign areas, decreased foreign-exchange earnings from the sale of goods and services to foreign ships, and foreign capital expenditures incident to the expansion of the domestic fleet. Freight revenues earned by domestic ships are credits to the balance of payments;[7] the other items are either debits or are neutral in their effects.

6. R. O. Goss, "Investment in Shipping and the Balance of Payments: A Case Study of Import Substitution Policy," *Journal of Industrial Economics*, XIII (March, 1965), pp. 103–15. Goss's model is frequently employed in discussions of this problem. See for example, Alex. Hunter, "Some Notes on National Shipping Lines: The Australian Case," *The Economic Record*, XLIII (March, 1967), pp. 20–46; Johan Seland, "Shipping in the Balance of Payments," *Norwegian Shipping News*, Special Issue, XXIII (June, 1967), pp. 57–66; and S. G. Sturmey, "National Shipping Policies," *Journal of Industrial Economics*, XIII (November, 1965), pp. 14–29.

7. Although revenues from the carriage of imports by domestic ships are

When imports are purchased f.o.b., the importing country is responsible for providing shipping services. Under c.i.f. transactions,
freight costs are charged to the exporting country, but they are
included as an element of the price to the importer. In either case, the
burden of freight charges is borne by the importing country. When a
country substitutes domestic ships for foreign ships in carrying its
import trade, a savings in foreign exchange results. Likewise, the
substitution of domestic ships for foreign ships to carry exports produces additional foreign-exchange earnings, as does increased activity
of the domestic fleet in cross-trades. Thus it can be seen that the total
revenues derived from carrying foreign-trade cargoes can be looked
on as a credit to the country's balance of payments, and the terms of
the export and import transactions, whether f.o.b. or c.i.f., do not
influence the final results.[8]

Merchant ships operating in foreign areas inevitably incur expenses
that must be paid in foreign exchange. Such items as canal tolls and
foreign port dues require full payment in foreign currencies. For other
cost elements, such as wages, fuel, repairs, stores, and stevedoring
expenses, at least part of the payments must be made in foreign
exchange. The proportion of such items purchased abroad varies. For
example, ships from countries that are oil producers generally will
purchase less fuel in foreign ports than will those from countries that
do not produce oil. But even the former will not buy all of their fuel
in home ports. Similarly, the extent to which repairs will be carried
out in foreign ports will depend to some extent on the repair facilities
available in the country of registry and will vary among different
countries accordingly.

Expenditures of foreign exchange incident to the operating of
merchant vessels in foreign voyages can be minimized by measures
designed to encourage the purchase in the home market of the largest
possible share of the goods and services required. Discriminatory
controls on expenditures for such items as fuel, wages, and ship stores

---

normally excluded from the balance of payments because they are in domestic
currency, they are included in the net effect on the balance of payments of the
substitution of domestic ships for foreign ships. This is done because the revenues
in question are equivalent to the foreign exchange formerly paid to foreign ships
for carrying similar quantities of imports.

8. Freight rates earned by the domestic ships are assumed to be equal to those
earned by the foreign ships replaced.

may depress foreign-exchange costs below what they would be in the absence of such controls, but they cannot eliminate them.

A significant part of the operating expenses of ships engaged in international trade will, therefore, entail foreign-exchange expenditures. The proportion of operation expenses involving foreign exchange will be higher for ships engaged in cross-trades.

When a country substitutes domestic ships for foreign ships to carry its sea-borne trade, increased expenditures by the domestic ships in home ports do not directly influence the balance of payments, but foreign-exchange revenues derived from the sale of goods and services to foreign ships are reduced.

It follows from the above that though the foreign-exchange revenue earned by merchant ships in foreign voyages represents a credit to the country's balance of payments, both the increased spending abroad, which the operation of merchant vessels in foreign voyages necessitates, and the reduction in foreign-exchange earnings from foreign vessels in the country's ports constitute debits to that account.

The final factor to be considered in determining the impact on the balance of payments of substituting domestic for foreign ships concerns the location of capital expenditures. Importing ships involves large outflows of foreign exchange, although the effects of these expenditures on the balance of payments in any one year may be mitigated somewhat by credit arrangements. If ships are built entirely at home, the balance of payments is not affected. This is seldom the case, however, because even countries with well-developed shipbuilding industries frequently import some ship components, as well as paying license fees for the right to produce foreign-designed components. The acquisition of merchant vessels does, therefore, almost always require some foreign-exchange expenditures, and such expenditures can be very large.

Effects on Soviet Balance of Payments

The methodology described above can be used to compare the estimated foreign-exchange earnings of the Soviet merchant fleet with foreign-exchange expenditures and the reduced foreign-exchange revenues likely to arise as a consequence of replacing foreign ships with Soviet ships. The results of this comparison show the net effect on the balance of payments in a given year of using domestic instead of foreign ships in moving a given volume of foreign-trade cargo and provide a basis for measuring the effectiveness of expanding merchant shipping from the standpoint of import substitution.

The hard-currency earnings of the Soviet merchant fleet have special significance for the country's balance of payments. Moreover, the conditions of payment for merchant ships imported from hard-currency countries are different from those for ships imported from soft-currency countries. For these reasons the gains and losses to the Soviet balance of payments generated by the merchant fleet have been estimated separately for hard currencies and soft currencies. Table 20 shows a comparison of the estimated gains and losses for 1966 in soft currencies, and Table 22 presents a similar comparison for hard currencies.[9] Columns 1 and 2 in Tables 20 and 22 show the debits and credits to the Soviet merchant-shipping account from carrying foreign-trade cargoes. Columns 3–6 show the gains and losses to the Soviet balance of payments from using Soviet rather than foreign ships in these operations.

The freight revenues earned in foreign-trade shipping (column 2) represent gains to the balance of payments (column 3). They include

9. The noncapital foreign-exchange expenditures and total receipts of the Soviet merchant fleet in foreign-trade operations were divided between soft currencies and hard currencies on the basis of the relative physical volumes of Soviet sea-borne trade with these two groups of countries. The physical volume of trade with each of the two groups of countries was estimated by relating it to the ruble value of trade with the same countries. The share of that trade moving by sea routes was estimated on the basis of the geographic location of the countries concerned and the commodity composition of the trade, since either or both of these factors may indicate whether alternative means of transport exist or are feasible. The estimated geographic distribution of Soviet sea-borne foreign trade is shown in Table A-7 in the appendix.

The estimated volumes of Soviet trade with hard-currency and soft-currency countries (Table A-7) indicate the following percentage relationship between hard-currency and soft-currency receipts and noncapital expenditures by the Soviet merchant fleet.

	Soft Currency	Hard Currency
1960	69	31
1964	63	37
1965	65	35
1966	63	37

Capital expenditures for imported merchant ships were estimated from data reported in statistical publications of the Soviet government as indicated in the footnotes to Tables 20 and 22.

TABLE 20. The Balance-of-Payments Effects of Using Soviet Rather than Foreign Ships to Carry Part of Soviet Sea-Borne Foreign trade—Soft Currencies, 1966

(millions of rubles)

		Gains		Losses		
	Debit[a] (1)	Credit[b] (2)	(3)[c]	Increased Spending[d] (4)	Decreased Revenue[e] (5)	Total (6)
Freight revenue		328.2	328.2			
Operating costs:						
Labor	62.0			4.2	1.4	5.6
Fuel	52.1			1.6	.5	2.1
Maintenance	24.8			.4	.1	.5
Stores	12.4			.7	.2	.9
Navigation	24.8			12.6	3.9	16.5
Administration	12.4					
Stevedoring	7.6			3.7	1.2	4.9
Sub Total				23.2	7.3	30.5
Capital costs	171.0			171.0		171.0
Total				194.2	7.3	201.5

a. Values for various elements of operating costs (excluding stevedoring) were derived by multiplying total expenditures in foreign voyages (column 6 in Table A-3) by the percentage of total costs accounted for by that element in 1963 (Table 2), and by multiplying the result by the share of the total sea-borne trade accounted for by sea-borne trade with soft-currency countries (Table A-7). Stevedoring expenses were estimated on the basis of their percentage share of total foreign-exchange expenditure by the maritime fleet; see footnote[c]. Capital costs were estimated from reported data on Soviet imports of merchant ships and marine equipment from soft-currency countries with the assumption that Soviet payment for such imports was on current account and that no interest charges were accrued. On the basis of deliveries of merchant ships reported in U.S. Department of Commerce Maritime Administration, New Ship Construction (Washington: United States Department of Commerce 1963–67), and various shipping journals, the share of merchant ships in Soviet imports of ships and marine equipment from soft-currency countries (Table A-8) has been estimated as follows: Poland, 60 percent; East Germany, Hungary, Rumania, and Bulgaria, 25 percent; Finland, 50 percent; Yugoslavia, 100 percent; and Czechoslovakia, 0 percent.

b. Income from foreign shipments (column 5 in Table A-6) multiplied by the share of total sea-borne trade accounted for by sea-borne trade with soft-currency countries (Table A-7).

c. Includes in addition to foreign-exchange revenues from the carriage of exports and cargoes in the cross trades, an amount equivalent to the foreign exchange that would have been expended if foreign ships had carried the import cargoes actually carried in Soviet ships.

TABLE 21. The Balance-of-Payments Effects of Using Soviet Rather Than Foreign Ships to Carry Part of Soviet Sea-Borne Foreign Trade—Soft Currencies, 1960 and 1964–1966[a]

(millions of rubles)

	Gains[b]	Losses		
	Income from Freight	Increased Spending	Decreased Revenue	Total
1960				
Freight revenue	105.0			
Operating costs		15.9	2.3	18.2
Capital costs		106.4		106.4
Total	105.0	122.3	2.3	124.6
1964				
Freight revenue	239.8			
Operating costs		22.1	5.6	27.7
Capital costs		104.7		104.7
Total	239.8	126.8	5.6	132.4
1965				
Freight revenue	300.6			
Operating costs		24.1	6.6	30.7
Capital costs		175.3		175.3
Total	300.6	198.7	6.6	206.0
1966				
Freight revenue	328.2			
Operating costs		23.2	7.3	30.5
Capital costs		171.0		171.0
Total	328.2	194.2	7.3	201.5

a. See Table 20 for sources.
b. See footnote [c], Table 20.

d. Foreign-exchange expenditures by the merchant fleet (column 7 in Table A-3), except for capital expenditures, adjusted to show the share accounted for in trade with soft-currency countries. The distribution of foreign exchange expenditures by the merchant fleet is given for 1963 in S. F. Koryakin and I. L. Bernshtein, *Ekonomika morskogo transporta* (2nd ed.; Moscow: Transport, 1964), p. 420.

e. Reduced foreign-exchange revenues for each item of expenditures (except for capital costs) assumed to be equal to extra foreign-exchange expenditures for that item for all Soviet merchant shipping. Since the largest share of the ships replaced in Soviet ports were from hard-currency countries, however, 80 percent of the decreased revenues have been assumed to be in hard currencies and only 20 percent in soft currencies.

TABLE 22. *The Balance-of-Payments Effects of Using Soviet Rather Than Foreign Ships to Carry Part of Soviet Sea-borne Foreign Trade—Hard Currencies, 1966*

(millions of rubles)

		Gains		Losses		
	Debit[a] (1)	Credit[b] (2)	(3)[c]	Increased Spending[d] (4)	Decreased Revenue[e] (5)	Total (6)
Freight revenue		192.8	192.8			
Operating costs						
Labor	36.4			2.5	5.4	7.9
Fuel	30.6			1.0	2.1	3.1
Maintenance	14.6			.2	.5	.7
Stores	7.3			.4	.9	1.3
Navigation	14.6			7.4	15.5	22.9
Administration	7.3					
Stevedoring	4.4			2.2	4.8	7.0
Sub total				13.7	29.2	42.9
Capital costs[f]	43.7			43.7		43.7
Total				57.4	29.2	86.6

a. See footnote [a] to Table 20. Operating costs adjusted to show share of the total accounted for by sea-borne trade with hard-currency countries.

b. See footnote [b] to Table 20. Revenues adjusted to show share accounted for by sea-borne trade with hard-currency countries.

c. See footnote [c] to Table 20.

d. See footnote [d] to Table 20. Increased spending adjusted to show share accounted for by sea-borne trade with hard-currency countries.

e. See footnote [e] to Table 20.

f. See footnote [a] to Table 20. Imports of merchant ships from hard-currency countries have been estimated as follows (in millions of rubles):

1955	24.0	1959	17.0	1963	51.2
1956	43.0	1960	30.9	1964	71.2
1957	22.0	1961	22.4	1965	42.5
1958	16.0	1962	46.3		

There were no imports of merchant ships from hard-currency countries in 1966. In 1960–65 Soviet imports of merchant ships accounted for about one-half of the reported value of imports of ships and marine equipment from hard-currency countries (Table A-8). Accordingly, imports of ships were estimated at 50 per cent of the value of imports of ships and marine equipment for the years 1955–59. Annual capital costs have been estimated on the basis of payment terms for imported merchant ships of 15 percent cash with the balance paid in seven equal annual installments with a 6 percent interest charge on the unpaid balance.

the foreign exchange earned in carrying exports and cargo in the cross-trades as well as domestic currency earned in carrying imports.

The latter is equivalent to the foreign-exchange debit on the balance of payments that would have taken place if foreign ships had carried the imports. Operating and capital costs are shown in column 1. Part of these expenditures result in losses to the balance of payments since they must be made abroad (column 4) and since replacing foreign ships with Soviet ships reduces foreign-exchange revenues (column 5).

The Soviets have attempted to keep the share of voyage operating costs represented by foreign-exchange expenditures (column 4) at a minimum. The location of expenditures for such items as wages, fuel, maintenance, and stores is subject to a degree of control. But the location of navigation expenses including port dues, tolls, pilotage fees, and charges for various other services cannot be shifted. Comparisons of the share of voyage operating costs paid in foreign exchange by the Soviet Union and by other countries suggest that the Soviets have been successful—largely by applying discriminatory controls—in maintaining foreign-exchange expenditures for these purposes at a minimum. In his analysis of the effects on the British balance of payments of a representative British dry-cargo vessel, for example, R. O. Goss estimated that 50 percent of the costs of fuel, maintenance, and stores would be paid in foreign exchange.[10] The Soviet data show that in 1966 only about 3 percent of the cost of fuel, 5 to 6 percent of the cost of stores, and between 1 and 2 percent of expenditures for maintenance were paid in foreign exchange. Only in the category of labor costs are the comparisons close. Goss estimates that 10 percent of British labor costs would be paid in foreign currencies, while in the Soviet case it was slightly under seven percent.[11]

Hunter judged that foreign-exchange expenditures for operating a representative Australian dry-cargo vessel would have about the same relationship to total operating costs as the British, except for fuel, only 10 percent of which would be purchased in Australia because of relatively high prices.[12]

The Soviet Union is a major oil producer, and the largest share of Soviet merchant shipping involves ports on the Black Sea, where the lowest fuel prices prevail. It is to be expected, therefore, that a significantly greater proportion of the fuel consumed by Soviet merchant ships would be purchased in home ports than would be the

10. Goss, "Investment in Shipping," p. 133.
11. *Ibid.*
12. Hunter, "Some Notes on National Shipping Lines," p. 38.

case with British and Australian ships. But a much higher proportion of the fuel consumed by Soviet ships would be purchased abroad if the location of such purchases were chosen on the basis of least-cost criteria.

The lowest fuel costs for a voyage are determined not only by the prices of fuel in the home port and in the areas through which the ship will transit, but also by the variations in earnings that may result from different maximum cargo loadings when different amounts of fuel are carried. Thus, if fuel is less expensive in the home port than in any of the areas to be visited, voyage costs will be minimized by carrying sufficient fuel for the round-trip, provided that this does not involve a loss in earnings from reduced cargo loadings sufficient to offset the savings on fuel.

The low levels of Soviet expenditures for ship maintenance and for supplies and stores in foreign ports also are indicative of efforts to conserve foreign exchange. It is likely that in the absence of such efforts the shares of the costs of these items accounted for by foreign purchases would be significantly greater. Repairs of damages from accidents and equipment failures that occur in foreign areas are frequently less costly if carried out at the first opportunity rather than delayed until the ship returns to a domestic port. Since only 2 percent of the costs of current repairs and maintenance of Soviet merchant ships in 1965 was accomplished at the expense of foreign-exchange expenditures, it is probably true that much of this work was postponed until it could be done in home ports.

The success of Soviet efforts to minimize the foreign-exchange costs of operating the merchant fleet can be attributed in part to the fact that the chief index of plan fulfillment for Soviet shipping lines and for individual merchant ships—and the main determinant of bonus payments for ships' officers and crew—is expressed as the percentage relationship between operating expenditures in domestic currency and net foreign-exchange income.[13]

Since the net foreign-exchange income from a voyage is defined as

13. In other words, ship operators are encouraged to minimize the ratio of ruble expenditures to foreign-exchange earnings. This influence operates independently of whether or not the ruble is overvalued. The calculation of net foreign-exchange earnings does not include expenditures for capital imports or the reduced earnings of foreign exchange resulting from the operating of domestic merchant ships; therefore, it does not provide a true measure of the effects of merchant shipping on the Soviet balance of payments.

the difference between gross earnings and gross expenditures of foreign exchange, an incentive is provided to maximize the ruble share of total operating expenditures and minimize the portion accounted for by foreign-exchange expenditures.

Charges for capital represent a large share of the total costs of ocean shipping and the share of those charges that must be met with payments in foreign exchange is extremely important in determining the effects of shipping on the balance of payments. The results obtained by this analysis are, therefore, very sensitive to the assumptions made concerning both the magnitude and location of capital expenditures. The Soviets have acquired approximately two-thirds of their merchant tonnage through imports in recent years and the losses to the Soviet balance of payments from capital costs have cancelled a large share of the gross foreign-exchange receipts earned by the merchant fleet.

The capital charges in Tables 20 and 22 are based on estimates of Soviet imports of merchant ships derived from statistical publications of the Soviet government. Trade agreements between the Soviet Union and other soft-currency countries normally provide for bilateral balancing each year. Provisions exist in these agreements for so-called swing-credits, which may bear small interest charges, but these are generally not of significant magnitude. Soviet imports of merchant ships from the soft-currency countries are, therefore, believed to be balanced annually by Soviet exports of raw materials and/or other commodities. The arrangements with Yugoslavia and Finland differ in detail from those with the countries of the Communist trading bloc, but no evidence has been found to suggest that merchant ships imported from these countries are financed on a long-term basis. The full amount of the estimated value of Soviet imports of merchant ships in 1966 has been charged as a debit to the Soviet balance of payments in Table 20.

The USSR has been able to arrange long-term credits for merchant ships imported from hard-currency countries. The terms of payment for these ships vary between countries and over time, but the details available concerning these terms are very sketchy. In estimating the debits to the Soviet balance of payments arising from such imports, therefore, it was necessary to apply payment terms that were felt to be representative of those actually pertaining to these transactions, i.e., 15 percent cash with the balance paid over seven years at 6 percent interest.[14] These terms were applied to the estimated Soviet imports of merchant ships from hard-currency countries to determine the amounts of hard currency paid out by the USSR for various years. The results for 1966 are shown in Table 22.

Data are available permitting estimates of the gains and losses to the Soviet balance of payments arising from the operation of the domestic merchant fleet, as shown for 1966 in Tables 20 and 22. The estimates for 1960, 1964, and 1965 are summarized and presented together with those for 1966 in Table 21 for soft currency and in Table 23 for hard currency.

Table 24 shows the net gains (in ruble terms) of both soft and hard currencies attributable to the use of Soviet rather than foreign ships to carry a portion of Soviet sea-borne foreign trade during the four years covered in Tables 24 and 23. A negative balance is shown in net soft-currency receipts for 1960, and a small net gain in hard currency, resulting in a combined net foreign-exchange deficit for the fleet of 17 million rubles. By 1964, however, substantial net balances were earned in both soft and hard currencies. It should be noted that the net gains in foreign exchange grew relative to gross foreign-exchange revenues as well as absolutely. This was especially true of the net gains in hard currency, which increased to nearly 54 percent of gross hard-currency revenues in 1966. The combined net gains of soft and hard currencies amounted to about 44 percent of gross foreign-exchange revenues in that year.

The estimated percentages of total foreign-exchange revenues retained as net contributions to the Soviet balance of payments (the balance of gains over losses) are higher for each of the years 1964–66 than those calculated for the British and Australian studies cited above. The estimates for these countries showed that 35 percent of the gross earnings of representative ships resulted in net contributions to the balance of payments if these ships were built entirely at home, and 19 percent if the ships were built entirely abroad.[15] If imports accounted for a large fraction of the value of ships added to the fleet as in the Soviet case, the share of gross earnings retained as a net contribution to the balance of payments could be expected to fall in the lower

14. The 6-percent interest rate chosen is essentially arbitrary, and the results obtained would, of course, vary significantly with alternative rates.
15. Goss, "Investment in Shipping," p. 113, and Hunter, "Some Notes on National Shipping Lines," p. 26.

TABLE 23. *The Balance-of-Payments Effects of Using Soviet Rather Than Foreign Ships to Carry Part of Soviet Sea-Borne Foreign Trade—Hard Currencies, 1960 and 1964–1966*[a]

(millions of rubles)

	Gains[b]	Losses		
	Income from Freight	*Increased Spending*	*Decreased Revenue*	*Total*
1960				
Freight revenue	47.2			
Operating costs		7.1	9.3	16.4
Capital costs		28.2		28.2
Total	*47.2*	*35.3*		*44.6*
1964				
Freight revenue	140.8			
Operating costs		13.0	22.2	35.2
Capital costs		42.8		42.8
Total	*140.8*	*55.8*	*22.2*	*78.0*
1965				
Freight revenue	161.8			
Operating costs		13.0	26.2	39.2
Capital costs		46.9		46.9
Total	*161.8*	*59.9*	*26.2*	*86.1*
1966				
Freight revenue	192.8			
Operating costs		13.7	29.2	42.9
Capital costs		43.7		43.7
Total	*192.8*	*57.4*	*29.2*	*86.6*

a. See Table 22 for sources.
b. See footnote c to Table 20.

portion of the range between 19 and 35 percent. The higher percentage of foreign-exchange earnings retained by Soviet ships is, of course, entirely due to the success of Soviet efforts to minimize the share of operating costs that is paid in foreign exchange.

The rising trend in hard-currency earnings by the Soviet merchant fleet can be viewed in part as a successful effort by the Soviets to gain hard currency from commodity exports. This follows from the fact that a large share of the merchant ships acquired by the USSR in recent years was imported from soft-currency countries and paid for

TABLE 24. Net Effect on Balance of Payments in Hard and Soft Currencies of Using Soviet Rather Than Foreign Ships to Carry a Portion of Soviet Sea-Borne Foreign Trade, 1960 and 1964–1966

(millions of rubles)

	Soft Currency[a]			Hard Currency[b]			Combined Net Gain[c]
	Gains	Losses	Balance	Gains	Losses	Balance	
1960	105.0	124.6	−19.6	47.2	44.6	2.6	−17.0
1964	239.8	132.4	107.4	140.8	78.0	62.8	170.2
1965	300.6	206.0	94.6	161.8	86.1	75.7	170.3
1966	328.2	201.5	126.7	192.8	86.6	106.2	232.9

a. Table 21.
b. Table 22.
c. Sum of column 3 and column 6.

mainly with raw material exports. Since the Soviets have experienced difficulties in expanding their commodity exports to hard-currency countries sufficiently to pay for their imports from these areas, the hard-currency earnings of the merchant fleet have particular importance.

The relative importance to the Soviet Union of contributions to its hard-currency balances of the magnitude estimated in Table 24 may be judged by comparing them with hard-currency deficits resulting from commodity transactions. The following tabulation shows that although in 1960 the estimated contribution of the merchant fleet to Soviet hard-currency balances was minor, by 1966 it had increased to nearly 45 percent of the deficit in these currencies arising from commodity trade:

	1960	1964	1965	1966
Soviet hard-currency deficit from commodity trade (mil. rubles)[16]	243	482	198	238
Net contribution of Soviet merchant fleet to hard-currency balances (mil. rubles)	3	63	76	106

16. Joint Economic Committee, Congress of the United States, Soviet Economic Performance: 1966–67 (Washington: United States Government Printing Office, 1968), p. 98.

Unless these estimates are greatly in error, therefore, the contribution of the Soviet merchant fleet to the balance of payments in terms of hard currencies became sufficient to offset a large portion of the deficits arising from commodity trade with the West during the latter part of the period shown. Heavy imports of grain from the West in 1963–66 necessitated by low domestic output were a major cause of the large Soviet hard-currency deficits during those years.

Other Measures of Effectiveness—The Relative Gains from Shipping

Measuring the absolute gains to the balance of payments resulting from investments in merchant shipping does not constitute a complete test of the effectiveness of that program as a policy of import substitution. A comparison of the gains to the balance of payments from shipping relative to those from possible alternative programs would offer a more meaningful check.

A test of this sort can be carried out in general terms, at least, by calculating the ruble expenditure necessary for each dollar of foreign

TABLE 25. *Cost of Shipments of Freight Cargoes in Foreign Voyages of Soviet Merchant Ships and Foreign Ships under Soviet Charter, 1961–1965*

	Cargo Performance		Cost of Shipments		Total Expenditures	
	Soviet Ships[a] (bil. ton-km.)	Charters[b] (bil. ton-km.)	Soviet Ships[c] (rubles/1,000 ton-km.)	Charters[d] (U.S. $/1,000 ton-km.)	Soviet Ships[e] (mil. rubles)	Charters[f] (mil. U.S. $)
1961	116.1	142.2	1.29	.69	149.8	98.6
1962	130.0	145.0	1.31	.71	170.3	102.3
1963	185.6	141.5	1.29	.77	239.4	108.5
1964	244.0	129.1	1.14	.68	278.1	94.0
1965	318.7	108.3	1.02	.66	325.1	71.9

a. Column 1, Table A-5.
b. Tsentral'noye Statisticheskoye Upravleniye Pri Sovete Ministrov SSSR, *Transport i svyaz' SSSR statisticheskii sbornik* (Moscow: Statistika, 1967), p. 151.
c. Column 4, Table A-5.
d. Column 6 divided by column 2.
e. Column 1 times column 3.
f. Column 8, Table A-9.

exchange saved in substituting domestic shipping services for foreign shipping and comparing the resulting ruble-dollar ratios obtained for other items in the Soviet trade accounts.

Table 25 shows the costs of freight shipments in foreign voyages experienced by the Soviet merchant fleet in the 1961–65 period[17] and the costs of similar shipments in foreign vessels under Soviet charter. By holding the ton-kilometers of foreign-trade shipments by the Soviet fleet constant at the 1961 level and attributing the increments in such shipments in the succeeding years to chartering[18] (Table 26),

TABLE 26. *Cost of Shipments of Freight Cargoes in Foreign Voyages of Soviet Merchant Ships and Foreign Ships under Soviet Charter, 1961–1965*

(cargo performance by Soviet ships assumed constant at 1961 level)

	Cargo Performance		Cost of Shipments		Total Expenditures	
	Soviet Ships[a] (bil ton-km.) (1)	Charters[b] (bil. ton-km.) (2)	Soviet Ships[c] (rubles/1,000 ton-km.) (3)	Charters[d] (U.S. $/1,000 ton-km.) (4)	Soviet Ships[e] (mil. rubles) (5)	Charters[f] (mil. U.S. $) (6)
1961	116.1	142.2	1.29	.69	149.8	98.6
1962	116.1	158.9	1.31	.71	152.1	112.8
1963	116.1	211.0	1.29	.77	149.8	162.5
1964	116.1	267.0	1.14	.68	132.4	181.6
1965	116.1	310.9	1.02	.66	118.4	205.2

a. See footnote [a] to Table A-5, cargo performance by Soviet ships held constant at 1961 level.

b. See footnote [b] to Table 25, growth in cargo performance in column 1 of Table 24 added to column 2.

c. See footnote [d] to Table A-5.

d. See footnote [c] to Table 25.

e. Column 1 times column 3.

f. Column 2 times column 4.

17. Data on Soviet ship chartering are not available for 1966. The cost data for Soviet shipments in Table 25 excluded passenger traffic so that the bases upon which Soviet shipping costs and chartering costs were calculated would be more comparable.

18. Cargoes carried in Soviet vessels and in foreign vessels under Soviet charter do not account for all Soviet foreign-trade cargoes, a very large percentage of which is carried in foreign ships under foreign control. Including these shipments would add the same amount (in dollars) to Tables 25 and 26. The ruble-dollar comparisons, which are the object of this analysis, are not affected, therefore, by their omission.

comparisons can be made between the savings in rubles and the extra expenditures in foreign exchange that result. These comparisons are shown in the following tabulation, where line *A* shows the ruble and dollar expenditures by the Soviet Union for the mix of domestic and chartered shipping that existed in the 1961–65 period and line *B* shows the expenditures that would result with domestic shipping held constant at the 1961 level—but with the cost per ton-kilometer declining as in Table 25—and the increment in ton-kilometers attributed to chartering:

	Rubles *(mil.)*	*Dollars* *(mil.)*
A	1,163	475
B	702	760

Under the alternative program (*B*), 461 million rubles were saved at the expense of $285 million in foreign exchange. This indicates that to save one dollar in foreign exchange an expenditure on the domestic merchant fleet of 1.6 rubles was required.

A slightly different ratio is found if both the ton-kilometers of shipping performed by the domestic fleet and the costs per ton-kilometer are held constant at the 1961 level.[19] This comparison is tabulated below with line *C* as the alternative case:

	Rubles *(mil.)*	*Dollars* *(mil.)*
A	1,163	475
C	749	760

With the assumption of constant unit costs in shipping, ruble savings are lower (414 million) and the ratio of ruble expenditure to foreign-exchange savings declines to 1.5 to 1.

The ruble-dollar ratios for merchant shipping can be compared with those for other items in the Soviet trade accounts to provide an index of the approximate relative effectiveness of merchant shipping as a policy of import substitution.

19. The assumption of constant costs per ton-kilometer or of costs declining at a rate somewhat lower than the one experienced has some merit as a companion to the assumption of constant ton-kilometers performed, since the reductions in shipping costs in the Soviet merchant fleet in recent years have been due in part to the increases in ton-kilometers.

TABLE 27. Ruble-Dollar Price Ratios for Selected Soviet Imports, 1965

Commodity Group	% of Total Imports[a]	Ruble-Dollar Ratios 1955[b]	Ratios 1965[c]
Petroleum and petroleum products	.9	11.5	1.0
Coal and coke	1.5	17.1	1.4
Ferrous metals	3.9	5.5	.5
Nonferrous metals	.9	12.0	1.0
Chemicals	4.6	11.9	1.2
Wood and wood products	1.9	6.1	.6
Textile raw materials and semimanufactures	4.4	31.5	3.1
Food (except wheat and wheat flour)	13.5	12.0	1.1
Wheat and wheat flour	5.3		1.3
Other consumer goods	14.2	17.0	1.6

a. Ministerstvo Vneshnei Torgovli SSSR Planovo-Ekonomicheskoye Upravleniye, *Vneshnyaya torgovlya soyuza SSSR za 1965 god* (Moscow: Mezhdunarodnoye Otnosheniya, 1966), pp. 38–52.

b. With the exceptions noted, the ratios used are those calculated on the basis of Soviet quantity weights. The ratios for petroleum and petroleum products, coal and coke, ferrous metals, nonferrous metals, and chemicals were taken from Central Intelligence Agency, *1955 Ruble-Dollar Price Ratios for Intermediate Products and Services in the USSR and the U.S.* (Washington: The Agency, 1960), p. 9; the ratio for wood and wood products is the unweighted ratio for sawn lumber given in Central Intelligence Agency, *1955 Ruble-Dollar Ratios for Construction* (Washington: The Agency, 1964), p. 36; the ratios for textile raw materials and semimanufactures, food (except wheat and wheat flour), and other consumer goods are taken from Central Intelligence Agency, *A Comparison of Consumption in the USSR and the U.S.* (Washington: The Agency, 1964), p. 13; the ratio for wheat and wheat flour was calculated by comparing the average unit value of imported wheat as shown in *Vneshnyaya torgovlya za 1965*, p. 49, with the average procurement price for wheat paid to kolkhozes in 1965 as shown in Keith Bush, "Agriculture Reforms since Khrushchev," New Directions in the Soviet Economy, Studies Prepared for the Joint Economic Committee, Congress of the United States (Washington: U.S. Government Printing Office, 1966), Part II-B, p. 456.

c. The 1955 ratios have been adjusted to reflect the ten-fold reduction in domestic prices that accompanied the revaluation of the ruble in January, 1961. The ratios for petroleum and petroleum products, coal and coke, ferrous metals, nonferrous metals, chemicals, and wood and wood products have been further adjusted to account for U.S. price changes by use of the appropriate wholesale price indexes by major commodity groups and by stage of processing shown in *Economic Report of the President* (Washington: U.S. Government Printing Office, 1967), pp. 464–67. No adjustments were made in these ratios for changes in Soviet prices. The 1955 ratios for food (except wheat and wheat flour) and other consumer goods were adjusted to account for U.S. price changes by use of wholesale

Table 27 shows nine ruble-dollar price ratios for intermediate industrial products, food (except wheat and wheat flour), and other consumer goods developed by the Central Intelligence Agency, and one ratio calculated by comparing the average unit value of Soviet wheat imports in 1965 with the average procurement price paid by the government to collective farms. These ratios are applied to major groups of Soviet commodity imports. The lack of a ruble dollar price ratio for machinery and equipment constitutes a major deficiency in this analysis, since imports in that classification made up over one-third of total Soviet imports in 1965. However, the commodity groups for which suitable ratios were found accounted for slightly more than 50 percent of Soviet imports by value in 1965, and provide a sample large enough to suggest how the returns to the Soviet Union—in the forms of foreign-exchange savings—from expenditures on merchant shipping have compared with returns that might have been realized from expanded production of other prospective import substitutes.

Another weakness of the analysis arises from the fact that the ruble-dollar price ratios for shipping were derived by comparing Soviet shipping costs with the prices of shipping services in world charter-markets, while the CIA ratios shown in Table 27 reflect comparisons of Soviet and U.S. prices. Comparisons of Soviet prices with world-market prices for these commodity groups would be more suitable. If U.S. prices are higher (lower) than world-market prices, then the ruble-dollar ratios are lower (higher) than would be the ratios of Soviet prices to prices in world markets generally. The lower (higher) ratios would bias the comparisons against (in favor of) merchant shipping.

Detailed comparisons have not been made, but U.S. prices for the commodity groups shown are probably as low as or lower, on the average, than prices prevailing in world markets. Any bias that has been introduced, therefore, has likely been in favor of, rather than against, merchant shipping.

price indexes by stages of processing and for changes in Soviet prices by use of the price index for consumer goods shown in David W. Bronson and Barbara S. Severin, "Recent Trends in Consumption and Disposable Money Income in the USSR," *New Directions in the Soviet Economy*, Studies Prepared for the Joint Economic Committee, Congress of the United States (Washington: U.S. Government Printing Office, 1966), Part II-B, p. 525. The 1965 ratios have been rounded to the nearest decimal.

Of the ten ratios shown in Table 27, only one, that for textile raw materials and semimanufactures (3.1 to 1), exceeds the range of the ratios calculated for merchant shipping (1.5 to 1). One additional ratio, that for other consumer goods (1.6 to 1), falls within the range of the ratios for merchant shipping. Imports in these two classifications accounted for 18.6 percent of total Soviet imports in 1965 and for about 37 percent of the imports covered in Table 27. This suggests that commodities accounting for about two-thirds of the imports covered in the table offered prospects of greater savings in foreign exchange per ruble of expenditure than did merchant shipping. Such savings could have been realized only in the event that (1) increased domestic production (where feasible in terms of the limitations of domestic resources and technology) did not substantially alter international price comparisons, and (2) the import content of the increased domestic production of these goods was not substantially greater than the import content of increased shipping services. The use of Soviet prices as a basis for judging the relative merits of substituting domestic products for imports is, of course, subject to the qualifications discussed earlier in this study concerning the deficiencies of Soviet prices as indicators of real costs.

EARNINGS FROM MERCHANT SHIPPING

It was pointed out at the beginning of this chapter that the economic benefits of Soviet merchant shipping policy were to be evaluated largely in terms of the net contribution of that policy to the country's balance of payments rather than by measuring monetary returns. Money earnings, while not suitable as an index of economic benefits in a general sense, indicate the viability of the industry from a budgetary standpoint. That is, they show whether or not expenses have been covered, or whether budgetary grants (subsidies) have been necessary.

Soviet merchant shipping has been profitable—in that money earnings have exceeded money expenditures—since at least 1958 and perhaps longer. Data are available showing income, expenditures, and profits in Soviet merchant shipping for 1958, 1960, and 1964–66. Income reflects revenues from all cargo shipments, both domestic and foreign, and from passenger traffic. Expenditures are calculated in

TABLE 28. *Earnings from Merchant Shipping in Soviet Accounting Terms and in Adjusted Terms for All Voyages, 1958, 1960, 1964–1966* (millions of rubles)

	Total Income[a]	Total Expenditures[a]	Income over Expenditures[a]	Interest Cost with Rate at:			
				6 %[b]	7 %[b]	8 %[b]	9 %[b]
1958	261,5	946,3	15.2	45.4	53.0	60.6	68.1
1960	321.1	283.3	37.8	60.2	70.3	80.3	90.4
1964	627.1	503.1	124.0	97.4	113.7	129.9	146.2
1965	743.4	578.5	164.9	114.4	144.5	152.5	171.5
1966	861.2	651.1	210.1	128.4	149.8	171.2	192.6

a. Tsentral'noye Statisticheskoye Upravleniye pri Sovete Ministrov SSSR, *Transport i svyaz' SSSR statisticheskii sbornik* (Moscow: Statistika, 1967), p. 160.
b. Calculated from capital stock data in Table A-1.

Soviet accounting terms and include charges for amortization of productive fixed capital but not for interest.

In 1958 income exceeded expenditures by 15 million rubles or about 6 percent. By 1964 the margin had grown to 124 million rubles or approximately 25 percent, and by 1966 to 210 million rubles or just over 32 percent (Table 28).

The relationship between income and expenditures in Soviet merchant-shipping changes when costs are redefined to include

TABLE 29. *Gross Returns on Capital Stock in Soviet Merchant Shipping, 1958, 1960, 1964–1966*

	Value of Capital Stock[a] (mil. rubles)	Income over Expenditures[b] (mil. rubles)	Gross Return on Capital Stock[c] (%)
1958	757	15.2	2.0
1960	1,004	37.8	3.8
1964	1,672	124.0	7.4
1965	1,906	164.9	8.7
1966	2,140	210.1	9.8

a. See Table A-1.
b. Table 28.
c. Column 2 divided by column 1. The rapid increase in the gross returns on capital stock reflect increases in factor productivity that are discussed in Chapter IV.

interest charges. Table 28 shows the effects of imputing such charges to the estimated value of capital stock at rates ranging from 6 to 9 percent. It was not until after 1960 that the margin of returns over expenditures was sufficient to cover a 6-percent interest charge (Table 29). But by 1964 it exceeded 7 percent; by 1965, 8 percent; and by 1966 it had reached nearly 10 percent of the value of productive fixed capital.

COMPARISON OF SOVIET AND FREE-WORLD SHIPPING COSTS

The economic effectiveness of Soviet merchant-shipping policy may be further evaluated by comparing Soviet shipping costs with those of other major maritime powers. Such comparisons are made difficult by differences in accounting concepts and reporting methods, and by the nature of the Soviet price system. Published Soviet data relate, for the most part, to the global average of costs for the Soviet merchant fleet. Available cost data for Western shippers, on the other hand, pertain largely to individual vessels or firms. There are unquestionably significant differences in costs among various Soviet shipping lines, and comparisons between Soviet and Free-World shipping costs would be more appropriate if they could be made for the same routes, rather than between the average of all Soviet shipping costs and typical Free-World costs, as is done here. Moreover, since Soviet prices are poor indicators of scarcity values, shipping costs expressed in rubles offer a much less precise measure of real values than do monetary measures of shipping costs in Western countries.

Notwithstanding these difficulties, comparisons of the ruble costs of Soviet ocean shipments with the dollar costs of shipments experienced by various Free-World countries afford at least tentative indications of the relative costs of Soviet shipping operations and reveal the areas of comparative strengths and weaknesses in the Soviet program.

Table 30 shows the reported distribution of Soviet ocean shipping costs in 1963 and an estimated distribution of shipping costs that might be considered representative for Free-World shipowners for the same period.

The data in Table 30 reveal a high degree of similarity in the relative magnitudes of the various elements of cost in Soviet and

TABLE 30. Distribution of Soviet and Free-World Shipping Costs

(percent of total)

Items of Expenditure	Soviet (1963)[a]	Free-World (1965–66)[b]
Labor	25	27
Fuel	21	18
Depreciation	24[c]	18
Maintenance and repair	10	15
Port and navigation costs	10	8
Other vessel costs[d]	5	5
Overhead	5	9[e]

a. S. F. Koryakin and I. L. Bernshtein, *Ekonomika morskogo transporta* (2nd ed., Moscow: Transport, 1964), p. 400.

b. Carleen O'Loughlin, *The Economics of Sea Transport* (London: Pergamon Press, 1967), p. 116. The estimates are based on cost data for 100 ships operating in various parts of the free world.

c. Includes major repair costs.

d. Water, laundry, small stores, etc.

e. Insurance excluded.

Free-World merchant shipping. Where significant differences occur, as in depreciation, maintenance and repair, and overhead, they can be attributed largely to differences in accounting practices. The Soviets charge major repairs ("capital repairs" in Soviet terminology) to depreciation. The sums of depreciation and maintenance and repair are very similar in the two accounts, 34 percent in the Soviet case and 33 percent for the non-Soviet shippers. The remaining significant difference occurs in the item labeled "overhead." In the non-Soviet account insurance costs accounted for 8 percent of total costs. Since the Soviet accounts do not include insurance charges, they were removed from the non-Soviet accounts and the remaining items were reweighted accordingly.[20]

For purposes of international comparisons it is convenient to divide shipping costs into two classifications: (a) national costs, for goods

20. Soviet literature on merchant shipping is extremely vague concerning insurance costs. When f.o.b. cargoes are carried, the ship owner does not bear the cost of cargo insurance. When Soviet ships carry c.i.f. cargoes, the risk of loss or damage to the cargo, and to the vessel as well, are *apparently* borne as part of the operating cost—without a separate charge being listed for that risk.

and services purchased in the home country of the ship owner, the prices for which may vary considerably among different countries, and (b) international costs, for expenditures made in international markets for which all countries pay substantially equal prices.[21]

Soviet merchant vessels are manned by Soviet citizens, and labor costs in Soviet merchant shipping are national costs. Although it is not suggested that this policy was inspired by economic considerations alone, it appears to have been consistent with them, since Soviet labor costs in merchant shipping are apparently lower—in monetary terms, at least—than those of other major maritime countries.

Soviet manning scales (crew sizes) appear to exceed those of Western countries generally, but in some cases they may be lower. A recent Soviet study of manning problems in the merchant fleet, which concluded that Soviet manning scales are higher "as a rule and especially so for tankers," cited the following example:[22]

	Japanese	*U.S.*	*Soviet*
Tanker size (dwt)	60,000	50,260	48,000
Crew (number)	48	51	61

Large engine-room crews seem to account for the bulk of the excess manning on Soviet tankers. Deck crews are approximately the same size, and Soviet vessels employ fewer service personnel.[23]

Comparisons of Soviet and Free-World manning scales for modern dry-cargo vessels show a somewhat different pattern. Estimates by the U.S. Maritime Administration for manning dry-cargo vessels operated under French, Japanese, Norwegian, and British flags are as high, and in some cases higher, than those reported for Soviet vessels of similar type and size (see Table 31).

Average money wages in Soviet merchant shipping are somewhat lower than those paid to merchant seamen in the major maritime countries of the Free World. The average money wage in Soviet

21. S. G. Sturmey, *British Shipping and World Competition* (London: The Athlone Press, 1962), p. 266.

22. R. S. Rez and Yu. I. Brzhezhinskii, "Puti sovershenstvovaniya organizatsii truda plavsostava" (Ways of Improving the Organization of Labor Aboard Ship), *Ekonomika i ekspluatatsiya morskogo flota Trudy Vypusk* 70 (Economics and the Operation of the Maritime Fleet), Ministerstvo Morskogo Flota SSSR "Soyuzmorniiproyekt" (Moscow: Transport, 1966), p. 82.

23. *Ibid.*

TABLE 31. *Manning Scales and Monthly Labor Costs of Soviet and Free-World Merchant Vessels, 1963*

(value in dollars)

Country	Vessel Type and Size	Crew Size[a] (1)	Avg. Wage[b] (2)	Avg. Subsistence and Social Security[c] (3)	Total Labor Cost (2 + 3 × 1)
France	dry cargo 10,000 dwt	47	368	178	25,427
Japan	dry cargo 10,000 dwt	50	204	87	14,550
Japan	tanker 63,000 dwt	48	204	87	13,968
Norway	dry cargo 10,000 dwt	46	278	114	18,032
United Kingdom	dry cargo 10,000 dwt	52	265	88	18,356
Soviet Union	dry cargo 10,000 dwt	40	143	45	7,520
Soviet Union	dry cargo 9,600 dwt	39	143	45	7,332
Soviet Union	dry cargo 8,900 dwt	43	143	45	8,084
Soviet Union	dry cargo 7,800 dwt	46	143	45	8,648
Soviet Union	dry cargo 14,400 dwt	57	143	45	10,716
Soviet Union	tanker 48,000 dwt	61	143	45	11,468

a. U.S. Department of Commerce, Maritime Administration, Letter L25-23: 620, February 13, 1967, for France, Japan, Norway, and the United Kingdom; Ya. B. Kantorovich, *Ekonomika morskogo sudna* (2nd ed.; Moscow: Transport, 1964), p. 76, for the Soviet Union.

b. Maritime Administration, Letter L25-23:620, for France, Japan, Norway and the United Kingdom; Tsentral'noye Statisticheskoy Upravleniye pri Sovete Ministrov SSSR, *Narodnoye Khozyaistvo SSSR v 1965 g.* (Moscow: Statistika, 1966), p. 567, for the Soviet Union (converted to dollars at official rate of exchange).

c. S. G. Sturmey, *British Shipping and World Competition* (London: The Athlone Press, 1962), p. 301, for France, Norway and the United Kingdom; Japan estimated at 30 percent of total labor cost; see footnotes to Table A-2 for the Soviet Union.

ocean transport in 1963 was only about 54 percent of the average of wages paid on French, Japanese, Norwegian, and British vessels (see Table 31).

Even if Soviet manning scales are on the whole higher than those of other maritime countries (as the Soviets themselves claim), such differences appear to be offset by lower Soviet wage rates. Soviet subsistence costs and social insurance payments are about equal to those of the other countries examined relative to wage payments, and thus are lower in absolute terms. Over-all money labor costs in Soviet merchant shipping are, therefore, lower than those of the Western European countries and Japan (see Table 31).[24]

In principle, fuel costs are international costs to the Soviet merchant fleet inasmuch as bunkers are available in most ports and generally at equal prices to all buyers. The decision concerning where to take on fuel for a voyage could, therefore, be resolved on the basis of least-cost criteria. It was pointed out earlier in this chapter, however, that considerable evidence exists suggesting that the location of fuel purchases for Soviet merchant ships is governed less by efforts to minimize costs than by the desire to conserve foreign exchange, and that the Soviets appear to be willing, for the most part, to forego whatever savings might be achieved by purchasing fuel abroad to attain that end.

Variations in earnings resulting from different ratios of cargo to fuel may determine the least-cost location for fuel purchases in those cases where the amount of fuel carried constrains the amount of cargo carried. This condition is seldom reached for freighters carrying mixed cargoes since the volumetric limits for such cargoes are nearly always reached before the weight limits. For tankers and bulk dry carriers, however, the opposite is frequently true. When this occurs, it follows that the ship cannot simultaneously carry full cargo and full bunkers, and that revenues will be maximized by maximizing the ratio of cargo to fuel.

The optimum combination of cargo and fuel for Soviet tankers and bulk dry carriers would consist of carrying minimum fuel and maximum cargo on the outbound leg of foreign voyages in trades where relative fuel prices were such that purchasing all fuel in Soviet ports did not afford savings sufficient to offset the revenue lost from reduced cargo loadings, and provided, of course, that full cargo loadings were available for all ships in question.

Exports comprise by far the largest share of the physical volume of Soviet foreign trade. In 1965, for example, exports accounted for 86 percent of the country's foreign-trade tonnage.[25] Since Soviet exports are made up largely of petroleum and bulk dry cargoes, when

24. This comparison does not reflect subsidized housing, free medical care, and other nonwage benefits provided to Soviet workers by the state. Allowance for these items would increase Soviet labor costs relative to those of the other countries considered. It should also be noted, however, that similar adjustments should be made to Japanese wage costs.

25. *Vnesh. torg.*, 1966, p. 20.

Soviet ships take on sufficient fuel in home ports for round-trip voyages, maximum cargo loadings frequently are not possible. Because of the wide excess in the physical volume of exports over imports, Soviet ships generally return from foreign voyages with less than full cargoes. Freight revenues that may have been foregone by carrying a lower ratio of cargo to fuel than necessary are seldom recouped. The Soviets may, therefore, pay a double penalty for purchasing fuel solely in home ports. Operating costs are increased when ships trade with areas where fuel costs are lower than in the USSR, and freight revenues are reduced when optimum cargo-fuel ratios are not achieved.

Some notion of the effects on Soviet shipping costs of purchasing all fuel in home ports in order to save foreign exchange can be gained from a comparison of fuel prices in the major shipping centers of the Soviet Union and in areas of the Free World most frequently traversed by Soviet merchant vessels. These comparisons are complicated by the fact that Soviet petroleum prices include turnover taxes. The amount of the tax is not specified, but a report published by the Soviet Academy of Sciences on transportation expenditures in 1955 indicated that turnover taxes comprised about 18 percent of the expenditures of the Ministry of the Maritime Fleet for fuel used for cargo shipments in that year.[26] In the absense of an alternative basis for estimating the extent of the turnover tax on fuel, published Soviet petroleum prices have been adjusted downward by 18 percent (see Table 32).

It is apparent from Table 32 that Soviet fuel prices generally exceed those of the major Free-World bunkering ports. The lowest price for fuel oil in the Soviet Union—in the Black Sea–Azov region—is about 20 percent above the price in South America, which is the highest price shown for the Free World. Prices for diesel fuel in the Soviet Union are closer to prices in the Free World than are Soviet prices for fuel oil.

Table 33 shows price ratios for fuel in the three Soviet sea basins and the Free-World areas listed in Table 32. The ratios range from

26. Turnover taxes were reported at approximately four percent of the ministry's total cost of cargo shipments, and fuel (including turnover tax) for about 22 percent. Turnover taxes thus accounted for 4/22 or about 18 percent of fuel costs. Akademiya Nauk SSSR, *Transportnyye izderzhki v narodnom khozyaistve SSSR* (Transport Expenditures in the National Economy of the USSR) (Moscow: Izdatel'stvo Akademii Nauk, 1959), pp. 128 and 20.

TABLE 32. Fuel Prices in USSR and Various Bunkering Ports of the Free World, 1965

(dollars per ton)

	Fuel Oil	Diesel
Soviet Union[a]		
Black Sea–Azov	22.78	26.60–28.43
Baltic–Northern Sea	27.04	29.52–31.91
Soviet Far East	35.35	38.27–39.76
United Kingdom, Rotterdam,		
Antwerp[b]	15.50	26.94
Persian Gulf (Aden)[b]	13.44	25.77
Far East (Singapore)[b]	13.84	26.59
Caribbean (Aruba)[b]	13.82	21.70
South America (Montevideo)[b]	19.00	29.99

a. Prices in effect in 1960 adjusted downward by 18 percent to exclude turnover taxes. No significant changes occurred in Soviet petroleum prices in 1960–65. Fuel oil prices are for fleet mazut. Ruble prices converted to dollars at official rate of exchange. See footnote to Table 12 for source.

b. "Representative Market Quotations," *Petroleum Press Service* (London), XXXII (July, 1965), p. 158. Prices in effect in July, 1965.

1.2 to 2.6 for fuel oil, and from 0.9 to 1.8 for diesel fuel. These price ratios exaggerate the potential savings to the USSR from purchasing fuel in foreign rather than domestic ports, since such purchases in many cases would require departures from established routes and extra port time, thereby adding to operating costs. If Soviet ships

TABLE 33. Ratios of Soviet Fuel Prices to Those in Various Ports of the Free World, 1965[a]

	Black Sea–Azov		Baltic–Northern		Soviet Far East	
	Fuel Oil	Diesel	Fuel Oil	Diesel	Fuel Oil	Diesel
West Europe	1.5	1.0	1.7	1.0	2.3	1.4
Persian Gulf	1.7	1.1	2.0	1.2	2.6	1.5
Far East	1.6	1.0	2.0	1.2	2.6	1.5
Caribbean	1.6	1.3	2.0	1.4	2.6	1.8
South America	1.2	0.9	1.4	1.0	1.9	1.3

a. Mid-points of range of Soviet diesel prices used. See footnote to Table 32 for sources.

trading with Cuba were to take advantage of the relatively low fuel prices prevailing in the Caribbean area—at Aruba, for example—approximately two to three days would probably be added to the round-trip voyage from the Soviet Union. In cases where the price ratios are low, the additional costs arising from such delays—part of which would have to be paid in foreign exchange—might well be sufficient to offset the savings from lower priced fuel In most cases, however, it appears that the price differentials are large enough to afford considerable savings even with the additional costs incurred by the delays involved in bunkering in foreign ports.[27]

Capital costs in Soviet merchant shipping are international to a considerable extent. Merchant vessels account for by far the largest share of the capital assets engaged in this activity, and about two-thirds of the vessels added to the fleet since the mid-1950's were built abroad. Sufficient data are not available to permit detailed comparisons of the acquisition costs of vessels purchased by the Soviet Union and those of similar vessels built for non-Soviet clients. As noted earlier, however, the evidence at hand indicates that the prices paid by the Soviets for imported vessels probably have not been greatly different from those paid by other purchasers.

The costs of merchant ships built in the Soviet Union, on the other hand, appear to be comparatively high. The continued Soviet reliance on imported vessels to expand the merchant fleet tends to support such a conclusion. This is further borne out by comparisons of Soviet and Free-World costs for constructing vessels of similar sizes and types. For example, the reported Soviet cost for tankers of the Sofiya type (47,750 dwt) was 8.0 million rubles—or $8.8 million at the official rate of exchange.[28] The estimated construction cost of a 47,000 dwt tanker (as of June 1, 1964) was $5.0 million in Japan, $5.7 million in Italy, and $6.2 million in the United Kingdom.[29] Similarly, the Soviet cost for a 30,000 dwt tanker was reported at $7.15 million,[30]

27. Fuel costs are, of course, a function of the quantity of fuel used as well as the price. It was pointed out in Chapter II that Soviet merchant vessels are, on the whole, relatively modern and efficient, and Soviet fuel consumption rates are probably at least on a par with those of other major maritime countries.

28. Koryakin and Bernshtein, *Ekonomika morskogo transporta*, p. 164.

29. American Committee for Flags of Necessity, *The U.S. Controlled Bulk Carrier Fleet*, A Study Presented to the President's Maritime Advisory Committee (New York: May 5, 1965), p. 49.

30. Koryakin and Bernshtein, *Ekonomika morskogo transporta*, p. 164.

compared to Free-World costs for a tanker of similar size of $4.1 million in Japan, $4.6 million in Italy, and $4.9 million in the United Kingdom.[31] Based on this limited sample, Soviet ship-building costs appear to exceed those of the major ship-building countries of Western Europe by 40 percent and those of Japan by as much as 80 percent. These comparisons are subject, of course, to the caveats mentioned earlier concerning the limitations of ruble prices as indicators of real costs.

The costs of maintaining and repairing ships, like the costs of building them, are international, since repair yards are located in most maritime countries and rates for repair work are determined independently from the vessel's flag of registry.

The Soviets apparently rely almost exclusively on domestic yards, however, to carry out repairs on their merchant vessels. This policy is probably based on the desire to conserve foreign exchange and/or other considerations not directly related to comparative costs, since Soviet yards appear to be both more expensive and slower than those in major maritime countries of Western Europe and Japan.

Port and navigation fees are international and the costs incurred by the Soviet merchant vessels for these charges are determined on the same basis as for other countries.

Miscellaneous vessel expenses include a wide variety of small stores and equipment that are probably largely national costs. There is no basis for determining whether Soviet costs for these items are high or low in relation to those of other countries, but in any case their share of total shipping costs (about 5 percent) is so small that anything but very large differences would not be of major consequence.

Overhead costs in Soviet merchant shipping are probably relatively high, but no basis can be found for quantitative comparisons with other countries. Here again, these costs account for only about 5 percent of total Soviet shipping costs, and unless they differ from those of other countries by a very wide margin, they would not have much influence on the comparative Soviet cost position.

The data underlying the comparisons of Soviet shipping costs with those of other maritime countries do not permit definitive judgments concerning the relative efficiency of Soviet merchant shipping. But they are adequate to support certain broad observations: (a) Labor

31. *The U.S. Controlled Bulk Carrier Fleet*, p. 49.

costs in the Soviet merchant fleet are lower than in Western Europe and Japan. This is due to low wage scales in the Soviet fleet. Soviet manning scales are generally higher than in the fleets of the other countries examined, but not by large enough margins to offset the lower wage rates. (b) The costs of acquiring and maintaining merchant vessels appear to be higher for the USSR than for Western European countries and Japan. The Soviets have imported about two thirds of the tonnage added to their merchant fleet in recent years. These ships were acquired at prices that were probably roughly competitive with prices paid for similar ships by Free-World countries, but the evidence on this point is inconclusive. It appears more certain that ships built in Soviet yards were obtained at somewhat higher costs. Soviet maintenance and repair costs also are relatively high, and since the Soviets rely heavily on domestic yards for this work—presumably as a means of conserving foreign exchange—their costs are thereby increased. (c) The Soviet merchant fleet apparently pays higher prices for fuel than do ship operators in other major maritime countries. Comparisons of Soviet and Western fuel prices are made difficult by the inclusion of turnover taxes in published Soviet prices. But if the share of published prices accounted for by turnover taxes was no greater in recent years than in 1955, Soviet prices for fuel oil and diesel net of turnover taxes were still substantially in excess of those prevailing in the major non-Soviet bunkering ports. Since the Soviet fleet operates almost exclusively on domestic fuel in order to conserve foreign exchange (especially hard-currency exchange) its fuel costs are relatively high. (d) For the remaining cost elements, Soviet costs probably do not differ from those of other major ship-operating countries by sufficient margins to have much influence on comparative cost positions.

On balance (and given the limitations of both the available cost data and the conclusions that can be drawn from them), it appears that Soviet labor costs are low enough in relation to those of other maritime countries to at least partially offset higher costs for capital, fuel, and other items. Thus, though the total costs to the Soviet Union of operating merchant ships are probably somewhat higher than the average of such costs in the other major maritime countries, and almost certainly higher than those of the more efficient Free-World ship operators, the differences do not appear to be inordinately large.

INTANGIBLE BENEFITS

The Soviet Union has derived certain benefits from its merchant-shipping program that, though real and perhaps even of dominant importance from the standpoint of policy, are not subject to quantitative measurement. These benefits are largely of a political and/or military nature, but they may have indirect economic connotations as well.

Since this study is aimed at measuring the economic costs and benefits associated with Soviet merchant shipping, the intangible gains arising from that program will not be analyzed in detail. The discussion will be limited to identifying the more important benefits in this group and calling attention to their more salient features.

Political Benefits

Soviet foreign economic policy cannot be considered independently from Soviet political policy, and much of Soviet foreign economic activity must be evaluated in terms of political criteria. The bulk of Soviet trade with Cuba and much of that with other less developed countries of the Free World, for example, appears to be conducted more for political than for economic gains.

The value of the merchant fleet as an instrument of Soviet political policy has been illustrated by the role it has played in enabling the Soviet Union to meet its commitments in Cuba. The levies that were placed on the USSR for military and economic aid to Cuba soon after the advent of the Castro regime in 1960 greatly increased the Soviet demand for shipping services. Since the USSR was initially unable to meet that demand with its own ships, it was forced to charter considerable foreign tonnage, particularly tankers. Efforts to deny Western shipping to the Soviet Union for this purpose, though not successful, apparently resulted in increased rates for tankers chartered from the Black Sea.[32]

32. National Petroleum Council, *Impact of Oil Exports from the Soviet Bloc* (Washington, 1962), pp. 519–20. A major Western oil company adopted the so-called "Black Sea Policy," effective July 1, 1960, under which Western owners were encouraged not to charter their tanker tonnage to the USSR. This study compared the rates paid by Western charterers for tankers with those paid by the USSR for similar tonnage during the eighteen-month period preceding the adoption of the "Black Sea Policy," and made similar comparisons for the subsequent

There is little question that the Cuban experience reinforced the resolution of the Soviet Union to expand its merchant fleet and reduce still further its dependence on imported shipping services. The importance Soviet leaders ascribe to the role played by the merchant fleet in support of political objectives is illustrated by the following statement by V. G. Bakayev, Minister of the Maritime Fleet, in 1965:[33]

Economic criteria, however, important as they are, still do not reveal fully the significance of the merchant fleet to the Soviet government. During the course of the Seven-Year Plan the merchant fleet of the USSR carried out a series of responsible tasks for the Communist Party and the Soviet government, which were not only economic, but also political in character. Paramount among these, it should be emphasized, was the participation in the breaking of the military-political and trade-economic blockade of Cuba established by American imperialism.

The Soviet proclivity for self-sufficiency has thus been a positive element in the decision to expand the merchant fleet. Though no longer pursued so assiduously as during the Stalin era, the ability to conduct its political and economic affairs as independently as possible from foreign influence is still of importance to the Soviet Union. The influence this consideration has exerted on Soviet shipping policy was indicated by Bakayev[34] recently, when in response to an interviewer's question, he said that the primary achievement of the Soviet merchant fleet during the Seven-Year Plan had been "the creation of a Soviet merchant marine, which has made it possible to free the nation from dependence on foreign vessels for maritime shipping. Today the Soviet Union can deliver cargo to any point on earth using high-speed Soviet ships."

The growth of the merchant fleet has broadened the ability of the Soviet Union to act in the international political arena. It has, for example, been an important factor in the program of economic and military aid to the less developed countries of the non-Communist world, which the USSR apparently is pursuing largely in an effort to

eighteen months. These comparisons showed that during the first period examined Western and Soviet charterers paid approximately equal rates, whereas during the latter period the Soviets paid premiums ranging from 3.4 to 29 percent. The aggregate costs of these premiums to the USSR was estimated at $8.4 million.

33. V. G. Bakayev, *Ekspluatatsiya morskogo flota* (Moscow: Transport, 1966), p. 14.

34. *Krasnaya zvezda* (Red Star), March 13, 1966, p. 1.

expand its political influence in those areas. The Soviet Union's preference for carrying cargoes under this program in its own ships is often cited as having contributed to the expansion of the merchant fleet. A recent publication of a committee of the United States Senate expresses this point of view as follows: "This new type of economic activity, to which the Soviet rulers attach high political value, has also tended to exert pressure for additional seagoing tonnage required to carry the cargoes. In order to reap, in full, the benefits of prestige and influence that flow from the foreign aid operation, the Soviet leaders understandably prefer to deliver these politically sensitive cargoes under their own control and at their own convenience; in other words, in ships of their own flag."[35]

Military Benefits

In addition to the political implications involved, the growth of the Soviet merchant fleet in recent years has created a range of capabilities of direct military significance. A merchant fleet is an important element of military power of a country that seeks to extend its influence to overseas areas. This arises primarily from the cargo-carrying capacity of the fleet and to a lesser extent from its ability to supply logistic support to naval forces.

The growth of the Soviet merchant fleet, therefore, has increased Soviet capabilities to use the high seas, but it has done little to extend its control over them. It has provided the Soviet Union with a secure means of transporting military cargoes to such countries as North Vietnam, Cuba, Egypt, and Algeria, but the limited Soviet ability to control the sea lanes over which these shipments must travel has not changed. This was illustrated during the Cuban crisis in 1962, when the Soviets were able to covertly transport offensive missile systems to Cuba in their own merchant ships. When the United States established a quarantine on the shipment of military hardware to Cuba, however, the Soviet merchant fleet became militarily ineffective.

The Preference of Soviet Planners for Stable Markets

Decision making in the Soviet economy is highly centralized, and the planning mechanism is geared to the attainment of prescribed

35. Committee on Commerce, United States Senate, *The Soviet Drive for Maritime Power* (Washington: U.S. Government Printing Office, 1967), p. 13.

goals within specified time periods. The meeting of a number of individual plan targets is important to the successful fulfillment of the more general plan goals. Failure in a key area can initiate a chain reaction that threatens failure in the whole program. Foreign trade, especially that with the industrial West, serves essentially as a time-saving device in achieving these economic planning goals. By importing more advanced Western technology, the Soviet Union is able to save the resources—including time—that would otherwise be devoted to the research and development of advanced techniques.[36]

The quantities and types of goods imported from the industrial West are geared closely to the requirements of the economic plan. Soviet exports to the West have persistently fallen short of the levels necessary to provide the hard-currency exchange to finance these imports, placing heavy pressures on Soviet gold reserves. Under these conditions, Soviet planners give considerable importance to their ability to predict the volume of foreign-exchange expenditures and receipts that will be involved in international trade.

International ship-chartering rates fluctuate widely in response to changes in supply-demand relationships. Dealing in such markets introduces an unwelcome element of uncertainty into Soviet foreign-exchange balances and makes accurate forecasting of these balances nearly impossible. Such uncertainty is viewed by Soviet planners as a threat to "orderly" economic processes and the successful fulfillment of plan goals; and its removal through the substitution of domestic for imported shipping services constitutes a gain to the Soviets, which, though not measurable in the usual terms, has an economic as well as a political content.

36. Penelope H. Thunberg, "The Soviet Union in the World Economy," *Dimensions of Soviet Economic Power*, Studies Prepared for the Joint Economic Committee, Congress of the United States (Washington: U.S. Government Printing Office, 1962), p. 430.

V

Alternative Uses
of Resources

This chapter provides an alternative indication of the relative merits of investment in merchant shipping. It involves an estimate of trends in the efficiency with which resources have been used in merchant shipping and a comparison of the findings with trends observed in other elements of Soviet transport and communications and in Soviet industry. The inferences that can be drawn from these observations are limited, but it is felt that they provide a useful supplement to the analysis of Soviet comparative advantage in merchant shipping in Chapter IV.

TRENDS IN INPUTS AND OUTPUTS

Output in Soviet merchant shipping—measured in ton-kilometers of cargo performed—increased more than fivefold in the period 1955–65. The growth in output was accompanied by an increase in the quantity of resources devoted to this use and by increased output per unit of such resources employed. It is possible to distinguish between these two elements of growth by constructing indexes that permit comparisons of the rate of growth with changes in the rate of increase in capital and labor inputs.

Indexes of output and capital and labor inputs are shown in Table 34. The index of output is calculated from published Soviet data

showing the ton-kilometers of cargo performed by the Ministry of the
Maritime Fleet in both domestic and foreign voyages.

*TABLE 34. Indexes of Output and Capital and
Labor Inputs in Soviet Merchant Shipping, 1955–1965*

	Output[a]	Capital	Labor[a]
1955	100	100	100
1956	119	114[b]	107
1957	134	132[b]	117
1958	153	148[b]	122
1959	166	170[c]	125
1960	189	219[c]	132
1961	228	249[d]	141
1962	248	283[d]	148
1963	323	322[d]	157
1964	425	366[d]	174
1965	554	415[c]	185

a. Tsentral'noya Statisticheskoye Upravleniye pri Sovete
Ministrov SSSR, *Transport i svyaz' SSSR statisticheskii sbornik*
(Moscow: Statistika, 1967), p. 159. The output index reflects
cargo performance in ton-miles, and the labor index is based
on the number of workers employed, hence both indexes are
measures of physical quantities.

b. S. F. Koryakin and I. L. Bernshtein, *Ekonomika morskogo
transporta* (2nd ed.; Moscow: Transport, 1964), p. 302.

c. S. Bayev, "Osnovnyye fondy morskogo transporta, ikh
ispol'zovaniye vosproizvodstvo, platnost' za nikh" (Fixed
Capital in Maritime Transport, Its Utilization, Reproduction
and Payment For It), *Morskoy flot*, XXVII (February, 1967),
p. 19.

d. Estimated at an average annual rate of growth of 13.7
percent, which was the average annual rate of increase given
for 1960–65 in source.

The index of capital inputs reflects changes in the value of the
stock of undepreciated fixed capital in maritime transport as of
January 1 each year. This is essentially a fixed-price index since it is
based on the replacement costs of capital assets in 1955 prices, and it
covers all fixed-capital assets in Soviet maritime transport including
shore facilities and "unproductive" capital. It is assumed that this
index reflects with reasonable accuracy changes in the value of that
portion of the total capital stock in maritime transport accounted for
by the merchant fleet. An index of capital services, which would

include working capital as well as fixed-capital services, would be more desirable for the purpose of this analysis, but the necessary data relative to working capital are not available.

The index of labor services is based on the average number of workers directly engaged in maritime cargo shipments. Since the average number of hours worked per week declined after 1960, this index overstates the growth in labor inputs in 1961–65, unfortunately the man-hour data necessary to correct the upward bias in the index are not available.

It is apparent from Table 34 that output in Soviet merchant shipping grew more rapidly than capital and labor inputs during 1955–65. The average annual rate of growth in output increased rather sharply in the latter years of the period while the rate of increase in capital inputs declined and that of labor inputs grew moderately. The following tabulation shows the average annual percentage rates of increase in output and in capital and labor inputs during the 1955–65 decade and for two subperiods:

	Output	*Capital*	*Labor*
1956–65	18.7	15.3	6.3
1956–60	13.6	17.0	5.7
1961–65	24.0	13.6	7.0

TRENDS IN FACTOR PRODUCTIVITY

Measuring Factor Productivity

The relationship between inputs and outputs can be further illuminated by distinguishing changes in the rate of increase in output that result from changes in the rate of increase in inputs from changes arising from other causes. This can be accomplished with an index reflecting changes in the productivity of combined factor inputs in the following geometric form:

$$I_t = \frac{P_t/P_o}{(L_t^a/L_o)(K_t^{1-a}/K_o)}$$

where I_t is the index value in year t, P_o and P_t are outputs in the base year and in year t, L_o and L_t are labor inputs in these years, K_o and K_t are capital inputs, and a and $1 - a$ are coefficients representing the relative weights of labor and capital inputs. The income shares earned by the capital and labor inputs are assumed to be proportional to their marginal productivities. The income shares for 1960 are used as weights to combine these inputs.[1]

The sum of the average annual wage, social-insurance deductions, and quarters and subsistence expense, multiplied by the average number of workers engaged in shipments, is taken as the return to labor in merchant shipping. As noted in Chapter III, the Soviet labor market is relatively mobile and the assumption that labor costs reflect the value of labor's marginal product appears to be reasonable.[2]

The return to capital is estimated by combining interest charges and amortization charges on gross undepreciated fixed-capital stock. Three rates have been chosen to illustrate the effects of varying levels in interest charges. The 6-percent rate corresponds to the rate used for calculating capital charges in Chapter IV, while the 8 and 13 percent rates were selected to match those assumed in a recent study of factor productivity in Soviet industry.[3] Amortization charges are

1. This index is mathematically equivalent to a Cobb-Douglas production function with neutral technical change, which may be expressed as $P = cL^aK^{1-a}$. If labor and capital are paid the value of their marginal products in the base year, it follows that the value of the coefficients are equal to their proportionate share of output in the base year. The production function may be converted to a ratio of predicted output:

$$\frac{P_t}{P_o} = \frac{L_t^a K_t^{1-a}}{L_o^a K_o^{1-a}} = \left(\frac{L_t}{L_o}\right)^a \left(\frac{K_t}{K_o}\right)^{1-a},$$

where P_t is the predicted output in year t arising solely from increased inputs, L_t and K_t are the labor and capital inputs in year t, and a and $l - a$ are the labor and capital coefficients (constant returns to scale). The scale constant c may be omitted in the index formulation. The difference in the rate of increase in predicted output from the base year to year t and that actually recorded provides a measure of the time rate of change in factor productivity.

For discussion of a geometric index of this form and its use in measuring factor productivity in Soviet transport, see Norman M. Kaplan, "The Growth of Outputs and Inputs in Soviet Transport and Communications," *American Economic Review*, LVII (December, 1967), pp. 1154–67; for discussions and examples of the use of a Cobb-Douglas function to measure productivity in Soviet manufacturing industries, see Raymond P. Powell, "Industrial Production," in *Economic Trends in the Soviet Union*, ed. Abram Bergson and Simon Kuznets (Cambridge, Mass.: Harvard University Press, 1963), IV; and James H. Noren, "Soviet Industry Trends in Output, Inputs and Productivity," in *New Directions in the Soviet Economy*, Studies Prepared for the Joint Economic Committee, Congress of the United States (Washington: United States Government Printing Office, 1966), Part II-A, pp. 271–325.

2. A correspondence between relative wages and relative marginal productivity in the Soviet economy has been assumed for other studies; see, for example, Noren, "Soviet Industry Trends," p. 303.

3. *Ibid.*

based on the rate applicable to merchant ships in 1960 (see Table A-3).[4]

Reliability of the Results

Table 35 shows indexes computed for combined factor inputs and factor productivity. The estimates of factor productivity must be qualified because of deficiencies in both the data and the index formula employed.

The index of output and the index of labor inputs are of a type suitable for making productivity estimates. The index of output reflects the physical volume of freight moved by the Soviet maritime fleet and the average length of haul. This index, therefore, is not incumbered by problems associated with aggregating dissimilar units of output, which are frequently encountered in measuring production

TABLE 35. Output, Input, and Factor Productivity Trends in Soviet Merchant Shipping, 1956–1965

(1955 = 100)

	1956	1957	1958	1959	1960	1961	1962	1963	1964	1965
Index of output[a]	119	134	153	166	189	228	248	323	425	554
Index of labor services[a]	107	117	122	125	132	141	148	157	174	185
Index of capital stock[a]	114	132	148	170	219	249	283	322	366	415
Indexes of factor inputs:										
6 % interest	110	124	133	144	167	183	200	218	245	268
8 % interest	111	125	135	147	173	191	209	230	258	284
13 % interest	111	127	138	152	183	203	224	249	280	310
Indexes of factor productivity:										
6 % interest	108	108	115	115	113	125	124	148	173	207
8 % interest	107	107	113	113	109	120	119	141	165	195
13 % interest	107	106	111	109	103	112	111	130	152	179

a. Table 34.

4. The coefficients for the capital and labor inputs are calculated from Tables A-1 (capital) and A-2 (labor). For the rates of interest used, the following coefficients are derived:

	Labor	Capital
6 percent	.54	.46
8 percent	.47	.53
13 percent	.36	.64

in broader economic sectors.[5] The index of labor inputs is based on the number of workers employed. It thus fails to reflect the reductions in the average work week that have occurred in recent years. This results in an upward bias in the labor index, which tends to damp the index of combined factor productivity for the years 1961–65.

The index of capital inputs is deficient in that it does not include working capital and hence does not measure total capital services. A much more serious weakness in this index arises from the necessity of applying estimated interest charges to capital stock. The higher the interest rate assumed, the higher the index of combined factor inputs, and the lower the index of combined factor productivity. Since the interest rates used are essentially arbitrary, the reliability of the values calculated for factor productivity is weakened.

The estimates of factor productivity are also sensitive to the period weights chosen for capital and labor inputs. If 1965 coefficients were used, rather than the 1960 coefficients shown in Table 35, the index of combined factor inputs for 1965 (with interest charges of 8 percent) would increase from 284 to 306, and the factor productivity index would decline from 195 to 181.[6] The increase in the index of combined factor inputs with 1965 weights results from the growth of the capital coefficient relative to the labor coefficient, and because the index of capital stock exceeds the index of labor services.[7]

5. Problems encountered in measuring aggregate output in Soviet transport are discussed in Kaplan, "Growth of Outputs and Inputs," and Norman M. Kaplan, *Soviet Transport and Communication Output Indexes, 1928–1962* (Santa Monica, Calif.: The Rand Corporation, November, 1964).

6. The assumption of neutral technical change (fixed relationship between coefficients) in the production function thus leads to biased results in the estimates of factor productivity. The use of 1960 coefficients apparently overstates productivity gains for the years after 1960 and probably understates them for the preceding years. These biases could be corrected by the use of coefficients appropriate for each of the years covered. Since income shares for some of the earlier years could not be determined, and in order to simplify calculation of the productivity index, the 1960 coefficients were nevertheless used.

A significant portion of the indicated increases in output per unit of factor inputs arose from purely technological changes, but changes in the scale of operations that were independent of technological changes also contributed to this trend. A discussion of the effects of changes in operating scale follows later in this chapter.

7. The labor and capital coefficients for 1960 and 1965 (with 8 percent interest charges) are as follows:

	Labor	Capital
1960	.47	.53
1965	.38	.62

The index formula used to estimate combined factor productivity deals explicitly with only capital and labor inputs. The reliability of the estimates would be enhanced if materials (largely fuel) could be treated in the same way as capital and labor in the index formula, but the data do not permit this.[8] Moreover, it is not possible to obtain a measure of output for Soviet merchant shipping that is net of material inputs, i.e., a measure of value added. Therefore, total output is imputed to only a portion of total inputs. The omission of the remaining inputs is not serious if it is assumed that such inputs are a stable function of output. This assumption would appear to be dubious, since changes in relative prices could readily lead to the substitution of materials for other inputs without changing the production function.

The available information concerning fuel consumption by the Soviet merchant fleet is not adequate to support time series similar to those for capital and labor inputs shown in Table 34. But scattered data do suggest that the share of total costs accounted for by fuel purchases apparently remained fairly constant over time, having been 22 percent in 1938, 24 percent in 1958, and 21 percent in 1963.[9] There were far-reaching changes in the use of fuel in Soviet merchant shipping during this period, including the greatly increased consumption of liquid fuel at the expense of coal. Higher average ship speeds tended to increase fuel requirements, and improvements in technology tended to reduce fuel inputs per unit of output. Nevertheless, the data cited above imply that, on balance, there was relatively little substitution between fuel and the remaining inputs.

Because of shortcomings in the statistical series and the index formula used, the estimated rates of change in combined factor productivity in Soviet merchant shipping shown in Table 35 must be viewed as approximations only. Notwithstanding possible inaccuracies

8. Raymond P. Powell argues against netting out inputs other than capital and labor and suggests a function with five separate input variables. See Powell, "Industrial Production." This point is also discussed in Lawrence R. Klein, *An Introduction to Econometrics* (Englewood Cliffs, N.J.: Prentice-Hall, 1963), p. 97, and by Carl F. Christ, in comment to Irving H. Siegel, "On the Design of Consistent Output and Input Indexes for Productivity Measurement," in *Output, Input and Productivity Measurement Studies in Income and Wealth*, Vol. XXV, National Bureau of Economic Research, Inc. (Princeton, N.J.: Princeton University Press, 1961), pp. 41–46.

9. S. F. Koryakin and I. L. Bernshtein, *Ekonomika morskogo transporta* (Economics of Maritime Transport) (2nd ed.; Moscow: Transport, 1964), p. 400.

in these estimates, it is clear that output grew much more rapidly than capital and labor inputs in the years from 1955 to 1965, and that this trend was accentuated after 1960. It is probable, therefore, that the removal of the sources of error identified would modify the estimates of combined factor productivity but would not reverse the trend shown.

The USSR publishes two indexes that measure the operating efficiency of the merchant fleet in purely physical terms. They are the indexes of (a) the productivity of cargo-carrying capacity, and (b) the coefficient of utilization of cargo-carrying capacity. The index of the productivity of cargo-carrying capacity, and to a lesser extent that of utilization of cargo-carrying capacity, have reflected positive trends in recent years, which tends to corroborate the trend in factor productivity shown in Table 35.

The productivity of cargo-carrying capacity is the most comprehensive measure of operating efficiency in physical terms. It relates the fleet's cargo capacity to the ton-kilometers of cargo performed during a given period. It is obtained by dividing the ton-kilometers of cargo performed by the fleet by the tonnage-days in operation of the vessels in the fleet.[10] Tonnage-days in operation is the sum of the products of the cargo-carrying capacity of the ships in the fleet and the number of days they were in operation.

The coefficient of utilization of cargo-carrying capacity measures the degree to which the fleet's capacity is employed, and it is therefore influenced largely by traffic management operations and the availability of cargoes. It is determined by the ratio of ton-miles of cargo actually performed by the fleet to tonnage miles. (Tonnage-miles refers to the ton-miles that would have been performed if all vessels had carried their full cargo capacity while in operation.)

These two indexes are published separately for the Soviet tanker fleet and the dry-cargo fleet. They are shown in Table 36 for selected years from 1950 to 1966. The index of productivity of cargo-carrying capacity reveals a sharp upswing that began in the mid-1950's and

10. The productivity of cargo-carrying capacity may be expressed as:

$$P = \frac{tkm}{TD} = \frac{tm}{(c \times d)_1 + (c \times d)_2 +, \ldots, (c \times d)_n},$$

where P = productivity of cargo-carrying capacity; tkm = ton-kilometers; and TD = tonnage-days, c = cargo capacity per ship, and d = days in operation per ship per year.

continued through 1966 for the tanker fleet, and through 1965 for the dry-cargo fleet. This trend reflects the increase in productivity in Soviet merchant shipping that resulted from changes in the size and composition of the merchant fleet and changes in Soviet foreign trade dating from the same period. It has also been influenced by improvements in ports, cargo handling facilities, and traffic management. Though apparently still far from optimal, these factors have not been so deficient as to constitute an absolute barrier to the improved efficiency of fleet operations.

TABLE 36. Indexes of Operating Efficiency of Soviet Merchant Shipping[a]

	Productivity of Cargo-Carrying Capacity (ton-miles per tonnage-day)		Coefficient of Utilization of Cargo-Carrying Capacity (%)	
	Tanker Fleet	Dry-Cargo Fleet	Tanker Fleet	Dry-Cargo Fleet
1950	68.6	44.0	51.3	58.9
1955	98.1	52.0	59.7	58.0
1958	104.3	60.8	56.2	58.1
1959	108.9	62.6	57.2	58.3
1960	117.7	66.1	57.4	60.3
1961	119.5	70.0	57.2	62.6
1962	119.5	65.1	55.4	58.4
1963	121.4	72.5	55.9	61.5
1964	128.7	74.9	55.6	61.2
1965	133.7	81.1	54.6	61.5
1966	137.1	78.9	56.4	61.3

a. Tsentral'noye Statistichekoye Upravleniye pri Sovete Ministrov SSSR, *Transport i svyaz' SSSR statisticheskii sbornik* (Moscow, Statistika, 1967), p. 151

No such trend is evident in the index of fleet utilization. In fact, by 1966 this index had declined somewhat from peaks reached at earlier dates (1955 for the tanker fleet and 1961 for the dry-cargo fleet). This index is influenced primarily by the availability of cargo and the proficiency of traffic management, which have apparently improved sufficiently to at least keep pace with changes that have been made in the size and composition of the fleet. The levels of utilization rates indicated by this index appear to be relatively high and are commensurate with a fairly high level of operating efficiency.

EXPLANATION OF TRENDS IN FACTOR PRODUCTIVITY

It has been established that the growth in output in Soviet merchant shipping in the period from 1955 to 1965 was accompanied by a sharp increase in output per unit of resource inputs. The increase in the ratio of the physical volume of output to the physical volume of resources used may be assumed to have been associated basically with two phenomena: (a) changes in the "state of the art" leading to technical progress, and (b) economies associated with expanded levels of operations.[11]

The index formula employed to estimate the rate of growth in output per unit of input contained an explicit assumption of constant returns to scale.[12] Under this assumption, the observed differential between the rate of growth in output and capital and labor inputs can be attributed solely to increased factor productivity arising from technological progress.

The assumption of constant returns to scale facilitates the analysis of productivity trends, but it is admittedly somewhat unrealistic, since part of the observed gain in productivity appears clearly to have resulted from the increased volume of merchant-shipping operations.[13] The dual effects on factor productivity of changes in technology and economies of scale can be shown by the following illustration. If the ships in the Soviet merchant fleet had been of the same technological level in 1955 as they were in 1965, but the output of the fleet (in ton-kilometers) remained the same, factor productivity would have been higher in 1955 than it actually was, but not as high as it became in 1965. The difference between the level of productivity that would have been achieved in 1955 (with 1965 technology) and that reached in 1965 can be attributed to economies of scale.

11. Other possible causes of changes in the rate of output to input, such as variations in the relative prices of inputs, probably had much less influence than these two.

12. In this formulation the labor and capital exponents sum to unity. This means that any increase in factor inputs brings about a proportionate increase in output. If the sum of the exponent exceeds 1, an increase in inputs brings about a more-than-proportionate increase in output, and defines a condition increasing returns to scale. The converse is true if the exponents total less than 1.

13. As indicated earlier in this chapter, as the scale of Soviet merchant-shipping operations has increased, factor inputs have been combined in changing (and apparently more efficient) proportions. Therefore, the assumption of neutral technical change constitutes an additional, but necessary, departure from observed reality.

It is not possible to measure separately the contributions to the growth in productivity from technological change and from larger scale operations, but the nature and direction of the influence exerted by major developments can be identified.

The addition of new, technically more advanced ships to the Soviet merchant fleet contributed to greater efficiency in resource use by permitting higher operating speed, by reducing crew sizes, by allowing faster and less costly loading and unloading operations, and by improving fuel economy. These new ships were also larger on the average than the older ships in the fleet, thus permitting greater cargo volume per unit of inputs and lower unit shipping costs. Productivity gains from these sources clearly may be classified as changes in the "state of the art." Gains accruing from improvements in the labor force and from better management may be grouped under the same heading.

Increases in the average length of voyage that accompanied the expansion of the Soviet merchant-shipping operations had a salutary effect on efficiency largely by reducing port time relative to time underway. As a result, both ships and crews could be more fully employed. This change may also be viewed as a technological improvement.[14]

Although technological progress of the type mentioned was of great importance, a significant share of the total increase in factor productivity in Soviet merchant shipping must be credited to the growth in the volume of freight cargoes carried by the Soviet fleet. When manifested in larger commodity flows on existing trade routes (as opposed to activity on new trade routes), the increased volume of cargo movement enhanced efficiency in several ways: it made possible higher load-factors, which reduced average freight costs by spreading fixed costs over a larger number of units; it permitted better scheduling, including the expansion of liner traffic, which tended to reduce port-time and benefit shore-based support operations; and it facilitated the use of larger and faster ships, which must be operated at high load-factors and with minimal port-time if the economies inherent in their design are to be realized.[15]

Factor productivity grew much more rapidly in the period from

14. This follows because it constituted a shift in the production function rather than a movement along it.
15. The introduction of such ships involved both technological change and economies of scale.

TABLE 37. *Factor Productivity, Output, Average Speed, Average Size, and Average Age in the Soviet Merchant Fleet, 1955–1965*

	Index of Factor Productivity[a]	Index of Output[b]	Index of Average Speed[c]	Index of Average Size[c]	Average age in Years[c]
1955	100	100	100	100	23.6
1960	109	191	108	110	15.2
1965	195	564	123	148	11.6

a. Table 35 (8 percent interest rate).
b. Table 34.
c. U.S. Department of Commerce, Maritime Administration, *The Soviet Merchant Marine* (Washington: United States Government Printing Office, 1967), calculated from Tables 1 and 2, pp. 30–33; 1956 used as base year.

1960 to 1965 than in the preceding five years. Output also expanded more rapidly during this period and more modern tonnage was added to the fleet at an accelerated rate. These trends are illustrated in Table 37. The increase in the average speed of Soviet merchant ships, and the decrease in their average age, serve as indicators of the modernization of the Soviet fleet.

COMPARISON WITH PRODUCTIVITY TRENDS IN OTHER AREAS OF THE SOVIET ECONOMY

The increases in output and factor productivity in Soviet merchant shipping become more meaningful when compared with trends in output and productivity in the Soviet economy generally and with those in certain sectors of the economy. Soviet GNP grew rapidly in the two decades following World War II, but the rate of growth declined after 1958, both for the economy as a whole and for nearly all of its major sectors. Merchant shipping did not experience a decline in the rate of growth in output after 1958, however, but continued to grow at an increasing rate. The comparative changes in average annual rates of growth in Soviet GNP, industry, transport, and merchant shipping for 1950–58 and 1959–64 are shown in the following tabulation (in percents):

	1950–58	1959–64
GNP[16]	7.1	5.3
Industry[17]	10.9	7.8
Transport[18]	12.2	9.8
Merchant shipping[19]	12.9	18.5

16. Stanley H. Cohn, "Soviet Growth Retardation: Trends in Resource Availa-

Soviet economic growth during the 1950's was marked by steadily expanding employment of capital and labor resources and also by a rapid increase in output per unit of these inputs. Declining rates of growth since 1958 have been attributed to the reduced rates of increase in the efficiency with which such resources have been utilized, rather than to lower rates of expansion of resource use. The average annual rate of increase in labor productivity for the economy as a whole dropped from 5.3 percent in 1950–58 to 3.3 percent in 1959–64, for example, while the rate of increase in employment in the economy grew from 1.7 percent to 2.0 percent between the same periods.[20]

In a study published by the Joint Economic Committee of the U.S. Congress, James H. Noren has demonstrated that the rate of increase in factor productivity in Soviet industry dropped significantly after 1958 while the growth rate in factor inputs remained fairly stable, showing only a slight downward trend. The average annual rate of increase in factor productivity in Soviet industry declined from 3.8 percent in 1956–58 to 2.0 percent in 1959–61. It increased slightly to 2.2 percent in 1962–65 and then fell again to 1.4 percent in 1964–65. During these same periods inputs of capital and labor in Soviet industry increased at average annual rates of 5.5 percent, 6.5 percent, 5.2 percent, and 5.6 percent.[21]

In a recent study of Soviet transport and communications, Norman M. Kaplan shows that both output and factor productivity grew less rapidly in 1959–63 than in 1950–58, and concludes that the decline in the rate of growth in factor productivity accounted for nearly all of the drop in the rate of increase in output in that sector. Kaplan's methodology for measuring productivity is essentially the same as that employed here and in Noren's study of factor productivity in Soviet industry. But rather than adjust published Soviet data to obtain esti-

bility and Efficiency," in *New Directions in the Soviet Economy*, Studies prepared for the Joint Economic Committee, Congress of the United States (Washington: United States Government Printing Office, 1966), Part II-A, p. 104.

17. *Ibid.*
18. *Ibid.*
19. See Table 34.
20. Cohn, "Soviet Growth Retardation," p. 105.
21. Noren, "Soviet Industry Trends," p. 292. Factor inputs estimated on assumptions similar to those used in estimating productivity in merchant shipping, i.e., labor inputs measured by the number of employees, 8 percent interest charges assumed, and 1960 weights used.

mated returns to capital and labor, Kaplan turns the problem around and calculates the values for the capital coefficient for which factor productivity grew faster in 1950–58 than in 1959–63. Kaplan's calculations indicate that for any capital share greater than zero the rate of increase in factor productivity declined after 1958. In other words, his conclusion of a reduced rate of increase in factor productivity after 1958 is independent of the relative weights assigned to the capital and labor inputs.[22]

The rate of increase in factor productivity in merchant shipping has not undergone a sharp downturn similar to that experienced by the Soviet economy as a whole and by most of its major sectors after 1958. On the contrary, after a brief decline in 1959–61 factor productivity in merchant shipping grew at accelerated rates in 1962–65. Table 38 compares the annual percentage rates of growth in factor productivity in Soviet merchant shipping, industry, and transport and communications during 1951-65 and various subperiods.

The estimated rate of growth in factor productivity in Soviet merchant shipping in 1956–61 was approximately equal to that for Soviet industry during the same period. In 1958–63 factor productivity in merchant shipping grew at 4.2 percent annually (Table 35), slightly faster than the yearly rate of 3.8 percent achieved in the Soviet transport and communications sector as a whole (Table 38). Factor productivity in Soviet merchant shipping grew at accelerated rates after 1961, averaging 8.4 percent annually in 1962–63 and 17.6 percent in 1964–65 (Table 38). The rapid improvement in the ratio of output to factor inputs was associated with a large increase in the volume of output. The ton-kilometers of cargo performed by the Soviet merchant fleet increased by 91 percent from 1955 to 1960 and by 195 percent from 1960 to 1965 (Table 38). The trends in output and factor productivity in Soviet merchant shipping after 1961 were in sharp contrast to those experienced elsewhere in the Soviet economy. As indicated earlier, the rate of increase in Soviet GNP—and the rates of growth in major sectors of the Soviet economy—declined after 1958. This decline has been attributed to reduced rates of growth in factor productivity. In merchant shipping, on the other hand, the rapid growth in output per unit of factor inputs appears in large part to have been due to the expanded volume of shipping operations and

22. Kaplan, "Growth of Outputs and Inputs."

TABLE 38. USSR: Average Annual Rates of Growth in Factor Productivity in Merchant Shipping, Industry, and Transport and Communication, 1951–1965

(in percent)

	Merchant Shipping[a]	Industry[b]	Transport and Communication[c]
1951–58	—	4.2	6.8
1956–58	4.2	3.8	—
1959–61	2.0	2.0	—
			3.8[d]
1962–63	8.4	2.2	—
1964–65	17.6	1.4	—

a. See Table 35.

b. James H. Noren, "Soviet Industry Trends in Output, Inputs and Factor Productivity," *New Directions in Soviet Economy*, Studies Prepared for the Joint Economic Committee, Congress of the United States (Washington: United States Government Printing Office, 1966), Part II-A, p. 282.

c. Norman M. Kaplan, "The Growth of Output and Inputs in Soviet Transport and Communications," *The American Economic Review*, LVII (December, 1967). Calculated from data in Table 3, p. 1159, with capital and labor coefficients used in estimating factor productivity in merchant shipping, i.e., .53 for capital and .47, for labor. Kaplan shows growth rates of 7.1 percent during 1951–58 with a capital coefficient of .4, 6.4 percent with a capital coefficient of .6. During 1958–63 the estimated rates of growth were 4.7 percent with a capital coefficient of .4, and 3.3 percent with a capital coefficient of .6 (p. 1165).

d. 1958–63.

increased lengths of haul, both of which contributed significantly to the increased volume of output measured in ton-kilometers.

Because of the nature of the index formula used and deficiencies in the data (which were discussed earlier in this chapter) the estimates of factor productivity in Soviet merchant shipping may contain significant margins of error. It seems unlikely, however, that such errors would be sufficient to account for the very rapid rates of growth in factor productivity indicated after 1961, or, stated differently, that the correction of errors that might exist in these estimates would result in estimated rates of growth in factor productivity similar to those found in the studies referred to earlier for Soviet industry and for Soviet transport and communications.

The striking improvements in factor productivity in Soviet merchant shipping resulted from the combined influences of relatively rapid changes in technology and output. Similar conditions in other industries could be expected to produce similar productivity trends. One may speculate, for example, concerning the changes in ratio of outputs to factor inputs that have occurred in the merchant fleets of other countries in recent years. Technological improvements have been evidenced in the merchant fleets of all of the major maritime countries as larger and faster ships have been introduced and as improved cargo-handling techniques have been employed. But the merchant fleets of these countries have grown at widely varying rates. For countries with rapidly expanding fleets, such as Japan, it is likely that the trends in factor productivity have been much like those found for the Soviet Union, whereas such improvements would be much less apparent for countries (like the United States and Great Britain) whose fleets have grown more slowly or have declined in size.

Rapid improvements in factor productivity in Soviet merchant shipping do not reveal the level of efficiency of resource use in that industry relative to alternative applications of the resources employed. The indicated increases in output per unit of factor inputs in this application have been rapid enough and have continued for a sufficient number of years, however, to suggest that any positive differential that may have existed between the rates of return to factor inputs in that use and in the Soviet economy generally (or in its major sectors) has narrowed appreciably in recent years.

VI
Summary

As the Soviet Union emerged from the recovery period following World War II, and particularly after the close of the Stalin era in the early 1950's, it expanded its international economic relations considerably. Soviet foreign trade grew more rapidly than total economic activity in the ensuing years and the Soviet trade coefficient (imports plus exports in relation to GNP) became larger even though in 1965 it remained the smallest (5.3 percent) of the major industrial countries.

In 1946 the Soviet Union had a small seagoing merchant fleet of about 2.7 million deadweight tons, including ships owned by the United States Government that had been transferred to the Soviets under lend-lease agreements. During the first decade after the war relatively small additions were made to the Soviet fleet, and by the end of 1956 it totaled some 3.4 million deadweight tons. In the subsequent ten-year period the Soviet Union expanded its merchant fleet dramatically—approximately tripling its size—and placed itself among the leading maritime powers of the world.[1]

The expansion of the Soviet merchant fleet laid claim to a large block of resources. From 1956 through 1970, for example, total capital investments in Soviet maritime transport amounted to more

1. U.S. Department of Commerce, Maritime Administration, *The Soviet Merchant Marine* (Washington: United States Government Printing Office, 1967), p. 30.

than 9 billion rubles,[2] and by 1968 more than 81,000 workers were engaged in transporting sea-borne cargoes.[3] A large share of the tonnage acquired during this period was imported, and many of these imports were from hard-currency countries. The question arises concerning whether the investment in merchant shipping represented an efficient use of resources consistent with other Soviet investment programs designed to maintain high rates of economic growth, or whether it was, as frequently viewed by Western critics, prompted largely by political goals that were pursued in spite of the economic costs involved.

The answer to this question lies in the relationship between the real benefits gained by the Soviets from the program and the real costs incurred, that is, the opportunities foregone in allocating resources to that use. This relationship can be measured in general terms by comparing costs of resource inputs with the estimated value of benefits. The data upon which these comparisons must be based are deficient in important respects and the results must be qualified. They are sufficient, however, to support at least broad judgments concerning the economic merits of Soviet investments in the merchant-shipping program.

Costs may be reckoned in terms of money outlays for inputs, but the economic benefits accruing to the Soviet Union from the expansion of its merchant fleet are more difficult to quantify.

The Soviet labor market is fairly mobile and relative wages may be assumed to correspond roughly to the relative contribution of labor to the value of output. Soviet industrial prices, on the other hand, are only tenuously linked (or not at all) to the supply of and demand for goods; hence, they are poor indicators of the real costs of economic activity. But if prices for the major material inputs in Soviet merchant shipping are adjusted to include interest charges on capital and to exclude turnover taxes from fuel, they provide a basis for constructing reasonable estimates of the real costs to the Soviet Union of the resources used in its merchant-shipping program.

Soviet prices are even less meaningful as measures of utility than as indicators of real costs, and the cash flows arising from merchant shipping do not adequately reflect the economic benefits the USSR derives from that program. For this reason, and because the Soviets

2. Table 4.
3. *Ekonomicheskaya gazeta*, No. 34 (August, 1969), p. 7.

themselves have placed considerable emphasis on balance-of-payments criteria in shaping their shipping policy, the effectiveness of the merchant-shipping program as a policy of import substitution serves as a good approximate measure of benefits. Comparisons of Soviet shipping costs with those incurred by other major maritime countries, and comparisons of trends in the efficiency of resource use in merchant shipping with similar trends observed in other areas of the Soviet economy provide alternative indications of the relative merits of investments in Soviet merchant shipping. Various intangible benefits —largely of a political nature—also must be included in the assessment of gains to the USSR from its merchant-shipping program.

Soviet shipping costs declined steadily with the expansion of the merchant fleet. This trend was reflected by both monetary expressions of costs and by indexes of real costs, i.e., by decreasing resource use per unit of output. The costs per ton-kilometer of cargo performed by the fleet dropped by approximately 60 percent from 1950 to 1965;[4] and the capital and labor inputs required per ton-kilometer were reduced by some 49 percent in the same period.[5] Money income from merchant shipping operations exceeded expenditures after 1958, indicating that the industry had become viable from a budgetary standpoint.

The cost reductions in Soviet merchant shipping resulted from technological improvements in ships and in shore-based support facilities, from changes in the volume and structure of Soviet foreign trade and to a lesser extent from improved managerial practice.

Crew sizes on Soviet merchant ships declined in relation to cargo-carrying capacity as the average size of ships in the fleet increased and as labor-saving equipment and techniques were introduced. The increase in labor productivity arising from these developments far outstripped wage increases, resulting in significant reductions in unit labor costs.

The addition of large numbers of new and relatively efficient ships in the Soviet merchant fleet reduced fuel consumption per unit of output. With the decline in the average age of ships in the fleet, the relative importance of repair and maintenance costs also fell. Soviet efforts to improve the efficiency of ship-repair operations contributed to this trend.

4. Table 19.
5. Table 35.

Changes in the volume and structure of Soviet foreign trade added to the improved operating efficiency of the merchant fleet. The growing volume of foreign-trade cargo carried on specific trade routes permitted higher load-factors and facilitated the use of larger, more efficient ships. It also contributed to the growth of shipping on regularly scheduled lines, and to higher utilization rates for the fleet as a whole. Extended voyage lengths accompanied the larger volume of traffic and tended to reduce shipping costs, as did increases in the relative importance of petroleum cargoes, which could be shipped at lower costs per ton-kilometers than most dry cargoes.

Although technological innovations made in the Soviet merchant fleet and changes in Soviet foreign trade have tended to improve operating efficiency, deficiencies in managerial practices had the opposite effect. Difficulties have been experienced in devising a system of material rewards that would induce individual and group efforts toward the ends stipulated by the central planning authorities without producing unwanted distortions. Errors in the central planning of cargo traffic have been the subject of frequent complaints in the trade literature, indicating that the effectiveness of this key management function has been far from optimal.

Efforts to ameliorate these difficulties included the introduction of new bonus incentives as a part of the wage reform carried out in 1960 and the installation of computer centers (beginning in 1966) as an aid in traffic management. The new bonus system shifted the emphasis for ships engaged in foreign voyages from maximizing gross output— as measured by ton-kilometers of cargo performed—to minimizing the ratio of operating expenditures in domestic currency to net foreign-exchange earnings. This practice facilitated more efficient cargo movements since under the old system ship operators could most easily fulfill their plan targets by carrying bulk cargoes, which are usually of lower unit value and carry lower freight rates than mixed cargoes. Cargoes of the latter type tended to be left to the residual carried by foreign-flag vessels.

The economic gains to the Soviet Union from its merchant-shipping program may be evaluated primarily in terms of the net impact on the balance of payments of substituting domestic ships for foreign ships in carrying the country's foreign trade. This effect may be defined as the net difference in the balance of payments from what it would have been if the substitution had not taken place. Accordingly, the net impact on the Soviet balance of payments resulting from the expansion of the merchant fleet can be estimated by adjusting the foreign exchange earned thereby for (a) increased spending arising from operations in foreign areas, (b) foreign capital expenditures incident to the expansion of the domestic fleet, and (c) decreased foreign-exchange earnings from the sale of goods and services to foreign ships.

The Soviets have been able generally to maintain foreign-exchange expenditures at very low proportions of operating costs. This success has been due in part to discriminatory controls on foreign-exchange expenditures for fuel and for other goods and services. Financial incentives to officers and crew to maximize the net foreign-exchange earnings of ships operating in foreign voyages also encouraged minimal outlays of foreign exchange. Efforts to conserve foreign exchange apparently have had precedence over least-cost criteria in determining the location of expenditures for such important cost elements as fuel and repairs.

In spite of heavy foreign-exchange outlays for imported ships, the Soviet merchant fleet has made substantial contributions to the country's balance of payments in recent years. In 1960 the losses to the Soviet balance of payments arising from merchant-shipping operations exceeded the gains by some 17 million rubles. This deficit was entirely in soft currencies, since a small positive balance was earned in hard currencies for that year. By 1964, however, the merchant fleet was earning substantial net balances in both soft and hard currencies. In 1966 merchant-shipping operations resulted in net contributions to the Soviet balance of payments of 127 million rubles in soft currencies and 106 million rubles in hard currencies.[6]

The rising trend in hard-currency earnings by the Soviet merchant fleet can be viewed in part as a successful effort to exchange Soviet raw materials for hard currencies, since the merchant ships imported from soft-currency countries are paid for largely with raw material exports. The Soviets have suffered in recent years from a persistent inability to market sufficient exports in hard-currency countries of the West to pay for imports from these countries. The deficits in its hard-currency trade accounts have placed a heavy strain on Soviet gold reserves. Hard-currency earnings by the merchant fleet, therefore, are of special significance to the Soviets. Net earnings of the magnitude

6. Table 24.

estimated would have been sufficient to offset a significant portion of the Soviet deficit arising from commodity trade with the West in the period 1964–66.[7]

Comparisons of gains to the Soviet balance of payments from investments in merchant shipping relative to those of possible alternative programs suggest that shipping was not the optimum Soviet choice for import substitution. Estimates of the potential savings of foreign exchange per ruble of expenditures in substituting domestic output for imports of commodities accounting for about 50 percent of the value of Soviet imports in 1965 indicate the existence of a number of alternative areas in the Soviet economy where the gains from import substitution probably would have exceeded those realized from merchant shipping. However, since these comparisons do not distinguish potential savings of hard currency from foreign exchange generally they most likely understate the relative gains from shipping. Soviet commodity imports from hard-currency areas for the most part are limited to capital goods desired to facilitate fulfillment of the economic plan and such consumer goods—largely grain in recent years—necessary to make up for short-falls in domestic production. The USSR has limited opportunities for correcting deficits in its hard-currency accounts by expanding commodity exports. This adds to the appeal of measures designed to increase hard-currency earnings through invisible transactions. Expansion of the merchant fleet has reduced expenditures of foreign exchange for the movement of Soviet imports and increased foreign-exchange receipts arising from the carriage of Soviet exports and cross-trade cargoes to hard-currency countries. Hard-currency expenditures for chartering ships to carry trade between the USSR and clearing-account countries also have been reduced.

Meaningful comparisons between the voyage costs of Soviet merchant ships and those of Western countries are made difficult by the nature of the Soviet price system and by differences in accounting concepts and reporting methods. Nevertheless, comparisons of Soviet outlays for the major items of expenditure—capital, labor, and fuel— with those experienced by countries of Western Europe and Japan provide a basis for a tentative appraisal of the relative Soviet cost position and permit areas of comparative strength and weakness in the Soviet program to be identified.

7. *Ibid.*

Capital costs in Soviet merchant shipping appear to be higher than for other major maritime countries. The Soviets have had some success in reducing cost by concentrating their efforts on series construction of a limited number of ship types, but continued reliance on imports for the largest share of new ship acquisitions suggests (even though it does not prove) a relative cost disadvantage in Soviet ship building. The Soviets apparently have been able to import ships at favorable prices, however, and have thus offset a large portion of their high domestic capital costs.

Labor costs in Soviet merchant shipping, on the other hand, are comparatively low. Manning scales for Soviet merchant ships are generally higher than in the merchant fleets of Western countries but this is more than compensated for by the lower level of Soviet wages. Although the wages paid Soviet merchant seamen are lower than those received by seamen in the fleets of other major maritime countries, they are high in comparison to other areas of the Soviet economy. Since the Soviet labor market is fairly mobile, the comparatively high wages paid merchant seamen insure an adequate supply of labor to the fleet. The quality of the labor force is enhanced by a comprehensive program of training personnel for a wide variety of positions.

The prices for fuel prevailing in major Soviet ports exceed prices in the principal bunkering ports of the Free World even after they have been adjusted to exclude turnover taxes.[8] The Soviets have shown a distinct preference for purchasing the maximum share of fuel in domestic ports—apparently from a desire to conserve foreign exchange, and especially hard-currency exchange—rather than taking advantage of lower-priced foreign fuel. By following this practice, they incur higher fuel costs than do ship operators who follow least-cost criteria in locating fuel purchases.

There is little evidence upon which comparative Soviet and Free-World costs for such items as supplies, stores, and general administration can be weighed. But in any case, expenditures for these purposes account for a small share of total costs and such differences as might exist are probably not large enough to have an appreciable influence on relative cost positions.

The comparisons between the major elements of voyage costs of

8. The most recent year for which the level of turnover taxes on fuel can be determined is 1955, when such taxes accounted for about 18 percent of the outlays for fuel by the maritime fleet.

Soviet and Free-World merchant ships are sufficient to demonstrate that on balance Soviet costs are probably higher than the average of costs among other major maritime countries. The evidence does not suggest, however, that these differences are of great magnitude. Soviet costs for capital and fuel appear to be higher, but they are at least partially offset by lower labor costs.

The expansion of the Soviet merchant fleet was accompanied by a clearly defined trend toward greater operating efficiency. This trend is evident whether measured by money costs or by relating physical units of output and inputs. Growing output per unit of inputs (rising factor productivity) in merchant shipping ran counter to trends manifested elsewhere in the Soviet economy after 1958. Beginning about that time Soviet economic growth began to slack off. This was true for the economy as a whole as well as for its major sectors. Soviet GNP grew at an average annual rate of 7.1 percent in 1950–58, but only at 5.3 percent in 1959–64, for example, while the yearly rate of increase in industrial production declined from 10.9 percent in the first of these periods to 7.8 percent in the latter period. Western economists have interpreted these declining growth rates more as the results of reduced rates of growth in factor productivity than as a consequence of slower growth in factor employment. Factor productivity in Soviet merchant shipping grew throughout the period from 1950 to 1965. This trend accelerated after 1960, as the fleet became more modern and the volume of cargo handled increased.

Sharp increases in output per unit of resources employed are not uncommon in new and rapidly expanding industries, and comparisons between rates of change in factor productivity in such industries and in older, more established industries say little about the relative levels of factor productivity in these different activities. The increases in factor productivity in Soviet merchant shipping have been great enough and have persisted for a sufficient time, however, to suggest that differences in the absolute levels of output per unit of input between this industry and other Soviet industries have been significantly reduced in recent years.

An evaluation of the benefits to the Soviet Union from investments in its merchant fleet must include not only tangible economic factors but also a variety of intangible ones, largely of a political nature. Western writers frequently have viewed the expansion of the Soviet merchant fleet as an integral part of a broader effort to extend Soviet influence abroad, particularly among the less developed countries of Africa, Asia, and Latin America. The existence of a strong Soviet merchant fleet is viewed as exerting a two-edged influence: It has enhanced the prestige of the Soviet Union and it has aided Soviet efforts to expand trade contacts with the less developed countries. The latter claim has some validity, and the Soviets themselves have frequently cited the contribution of the merchant fleet to the pursuit of political goals and to bolstering the Soviet position as a world power.

Whatever the dominant motives for the expansion of the Soviet merchant fleet were, there is little doubt that this program has endowed the USSR with a valuable instrument for implementing its foreign political policies as well as for seeking purely economic ends. This was best illustrated, perhaps, by the ability acquired by the USSR (which it did not initially have) to fulfill its commitments to Cuba without reliance on tonnage chartered from Free-World ship owners.

The growth of the merchant fleet has also enhanced Soviet military capabilities. This has arisen from the greater ability of the merchant fleet to supply logistic support to Soviet naval and amphibious forces and from providing the Soviet Union with a secure means of transporting military cargoes to such countries as North Vietnam, Cuba, Egypt, and Algeria.

The Soviet planning system is keyed to rather closely calculated resource balances. Imports, particularly those from industrialized countries of the West, are determined by the requirements of the economic plan. Anticipated foreign-exchange balances are thus key elements in the planning process. Reasonably accurate knowledge of the amount of foreign exchange (especially hard-currency exchange) to be available during the plan period, therefore, is of considerable importance to Soviet planners.

Charter rates for merchant vessels vary widely with seasonal changes and in response to random influences. Dependence on chartered vessels to satisfy a large portion of Soviet demand for shipping services thus added a considerable element of uncertainty to the projection of foreign-exchange balances. The removal of a large part of that uncertainty as a result of the reduced demand for chartered vessels must be counted among the gains accruing to the Soviet Union from the expansion of its merchant fleet.

In summary, the combined economic and political gains arising from the expansion of the Soviet merchant fleet appear to be sufficient to support the judgment that the program has passed the test prescribed for it at the outset of this study, namely, that the real value of these benefits has outweighed the associated costs. It is clear that the USSR possesses an adequate resource base to support an efficient merchant fleet and that rapid growth in Soviet foreign trade has afforded opportunities for these resources to be employed in favorable quantities and combinations. There is no evidence that Soviet merchant-shipping costs are greatly in excess of those of other major maritime countries, or that the Soviets have suffered appreciable economic losses from the decision to supply a large share of the country's growing demand for shipping services with the domestic fleet. It is also clear that investments in Soviet merchant shipping have yielded substantial economic returns, and that the rate of return from these investments has accelerated in recent years. The merchant fleet has made a significant contribution to the Soviet balance of payments and has aided materially in making up the deficits in hard-currency balances arising from Soviet commodity trade with the industrial nations of the West. Since the Soviet Union has limited opportunities for expanding its commodity exports to the West, the hard-currency earnings of the merchant fleet have been of great importance. The observation that alternative programs of import substitution possibly would have yielded superior results—at least in terms of total foreign-exchange savings—does not detract from this conclusion.

VII

Epilogue:
The Soviet Merchant Fleet
and World Shipping

It was noted at the outset of this study that the emergence of the Soviet Union as a major maritime power has occasioned concern and even alarm in the West. These apprehensions have been expressed largely by individuals or groups associated with the merchant-shipping industry, and by those who are more fearful of the political and military implications of this development.

Numerous press reports, magazine articles, and several reports by committees of the United States Congress have borne witness to the threats perceived to Western commercial, political, and military interests by the expansion of Soviet maritime power. An example of how vivid these perceptions have become has been afforded by Edwin M. Hood, president of the Shipbuilders Council of America, Inc., when he responded as follows to an interviewer's question concerning whether he saw anything more than commercial motives behind the build-up of Soviet shipping capacity:[1]

Yes. There has been no decline in the objectives of international communism. The dialect may have changed, but the goal of world domination has been reiterated with every change of command at the Kremlin. To that end, Russian shipping and shipbuilding are regarded as important

1. "An Interview with Edwin M. Hood," in *Marine Engineering/Log*, LXXI, No. 2 (February 1966), p. 51.

instruments of national policy, and the Soviet Union is moving rapidly to control the oceans and trade routes of the world. . . .

Because of her enormous fleet expansion program, the Soviet Union will soon be able to manipulate ocean freight rates at will, and through a superiority in terms of numbers of ships in-being and mobility, she will be on the road to economic domination of the world.

The foreword to a report on the Soviet merchant fleet by the Committee on Commerce of the U.S. Senate begins with the assertion that "Soviet Russia rapidly is emerging as a major maritime power, dedicated to economic, political and strategic objectives, and committed to disrupting and ultimately dominating world trade."[2]

It is beyond the scope of this study to attempt more than a very cursory treatment of the political and military ramifications of the expansion of Soviet maritime power. In assessing the economic threat posed by the Soviet fleet, i.e., its competitive challenge to Western shipping interests, certain factors that mitigate the seriousness of that challenge must be evaluated. Paramount among these are (a) the size of the Soviet fleet relative to the fleets of other major maritime countries and to the total world fleet; (b) the role of the Soviet fleet in carrying the country's sea-borne trade and the prospective growth of that trade in relation to the expected increase in Soviet shipping capacity; (c) the limitations on the competitive strength of the Soviet fleet imposed by the lack of certain types of ships and by exclusion from carrying U.S. trade cargoes; and, finally (d) the shipping policies likely to be favored by the Soviet government.

The Soviet fleet has grown impressively since the mid-1950's, but it still does not loom large in comparison with other major merchant fleets of the world. Moreover, the relative position of the Soviet fleet probably will not change much during the next decade.

Table 39 shows Soviet merchant tonnage and that of the other nine largest merchant fleets of the world at the end of 1968 as reported by the U.S. Maritime Administration.

At the end of 1968 the Soviet fleet comprised a little more than 4 percent of total world merchant-ship tonnage. The Soviets have projected an approximate doubling of the size of their fleet by 1980, to

2. Committee on Commerce, United States Senate, *The Growing Strength of the Soviet Merchant Fleet* (Washington: United States Government Printing Office, 1964), p. iii.

TABLE 39. Leading Merchant Fleets of the World as of December 31, 1968[a]

Country	DWT (000's)	Country	DWT (000's)
Liberia	41,141	USSR	11,911
Norway	30,593	Greece	11,543
Great Britain	29,917	West Germany	9,320
Japan	29,220	Italy	8,686
United States	15,346[b]	Panama	8,009

a. United States Department of Commerce, Maritime Administration, *Merchant Fleets of the World, Oceangoing Steam and Motorships of 1,000 Gross Tons and Over* (Washington: United States Government Printing Office, 1969), p. 6.
b. Excluding ships owned by the U.S. Government totaling 10,118,000 dwt.

22 to 23 million dwt.[3] By that time it could well surpass the privately owned U.S. fleet in size and become the world's fifth largest merchant fleet. It is not very likely, however, that the Soviet position will improve much with respect to total world tonnage. In the decade ending in 1968 Soviet merchant tonnage grew at an average annual rate of 12.7 percent, which was considerably faster than the 6.7 percent rate of increase in the total world fleet during that period. But the average annual rate of growth projected for the Soviet fleet to 1980 is lower (5.6 percent) than the rates experienced in the world fleet in recent years. The Soviet share of total world tonnage thus will not increase unless the rate of growth in the world fleet drops rather sharply. For example, if total world tonnage increases at only one-half the average annual rate in 1968–80 (3.3 percent) than it did in 1959–68, the Soviet share of total world merchant-ship tonnage will still be less than 6 percent.

Another factor to be considered in assessing the present and potential future impact of the Soviet merchant fleet on world shipping is the role of the fleet in carrying the country's sea-borne trade and the prospective growth of that trade in relation to the expected increase in the size of the fleet. The share of Soviet import and export cargoes carried in domestic bottoms has increased in recent years—from a low of 37 percent in 1962 to 52 percent in 1967 (Table 1)—but the country is still a substantial importer of shipping services, as the following tabulation of the tonnage of Soviet foreign-trade cargoes

3. "Dostizheniya, perspektivy" (Achievements and Prospects), *Vyshka* (The Tower), February 19, 1969, p. 2.

carried in Soviet and foreign-flag ships in 1967 shows (in millions of tons):[4]

Soviet sea-borne trade cargoes	124.0
Carried in Soviet ships	64.3
Carried in foreign ships	59.7
Carried by Soviet ships in cross-trades	15.7

The balance of Soviet foreign-trade cargo carried in foreign-flag ships over cargo carried in Soviet ships for foreign clients in 1967 was thus 44 million tons.

The USSR is seeking to increase the share of its sea-borne trade carried by its own fleet. Specifically, it hopes eventually to carry all of its c.i.f. exports and f.o.b. imports in domestic bottoms. It also intends to expand the carriage of foreign-owned cargo in Soviet ships as a means of earning more foreign exchange.

Continued progress toward these goals will probably be made during the next few years, but if the growth in Soviet sea-borne trade during the 1970's is similar to that of the 1950's and 1960's, it will absorb much of the increase in carrying capacity of the Soviet fleet and will reduce the margin left for enlarging the share of the country's foreign sea-borne trade cargoes carried in domestic ships and for chartering to foreign shippers.

The competitive impact of the Soviet merchant fleet on world shipping has also been limited by the fact that Soviet ships have not carried U.S. foreign-trade cargoes. For as long as threatened union boycotts and U.S. shipping legislation discourage calls by Soviet ships at U.S. ports the Soviet Union will be excluded from competing for a sizable share of world maritime traffic.[5]

At the present time the Soviet merchant fleet has no container ships, large tankers, or large, bulk dry-cargo carriers. A limited number of ships in these categories are to be added to the Soviet fleet during the

4. V. G. Bakayev, *SSSR na mirovykh morskykh putyakh* (The USSR on the World's Seaways) (Moscow: Transport, 1969), p. 25. Soviet sea-borne foreign-trade tonnage shown here exceeds that reported for 1967 by the "Soviet Ministry of Foreign Trade" (Table 1) by 15 million tons. The higher figure probably results from the inclusion of Danube River traffic and aid cargoes, which are not included in the Foreign Trade Ministry data.

5. The threatened boycott of Soviet ships by U.S. longshoremen apply to ports on the East Coast and Gulf Coast only. But Soviet merchant ships had not visited any U.S. ports for many years until late in 1969 when two Soviet freighters called at ports in the Pacific Northwest.

1970's, including a new class of tankers of about 150,000 dwt, and bulk dry carriers of 36,000 dwt. These ships will not be in service for several years, however, and in the meantime even larger tankers and bulk dry-cargo carriers will be added to Western merchant fleets.

The rapid expansion of container shipping and the addition of more supertankers to merchant fleets in the West will reduce the relative competitive strength of the Soviet merchant fleet. The world supply of ships available for use in the tramp trades and/or on noncontainer lines will be increased as conventional cargo liners are replaced by container ships. This could depress the market for ships of the type the USSR will have available for competition during the 1970's. As more supertankers are put into service in the West, many smaller tankers likely will become available for charter in the short-haul and low-volume trades where Soviet tankers are best able to compete.

Finally, but by no means least important, the competitive potential of the Soviet merchant fleet cannot be judged independently from Soviet shipping policy. This study is directed to the question of whether or not that policy has had a plausible economic rationale; that is, whether or not it has been worthwhile to the USSR in purely economic terms. The analysis in the preceding chapters supports an affirmative answer to that question. This affirmation does not, of course, prove conclusively that Soviet shipping policy has been inspired solely, or even in principal part, by economic considerations. But it does demonstrate that that policy has been basically consistent with such motivations. And it provides a certain amount of support for a hypothesis that economic criteria, especially the need to improve the country's hard-currency balances, have been the strongest *single* motivating force behind the expansion of the Soviet merchant fleet and have largely determined the way in which that fleet has been used. Moreover, no evidence has been found to suggest that this hypothesis will not remain valid for some time to come.

In seeking to gain admittance for their ships in trades where they have not previously participated, or in attempting to acquire a larger share of the cargo in areas where they are already established, the Soviets have sometimes used tactics that precipitated charges of unfairness by their competitors and gave rise to questions concerning their ultimate objectives. A notable example of this occurred in 1968, when the Soviets elbowed their way into the Australia-to-Europe Shipping Conference.

In the latter part of 1968 the Soviet Baltic Shipping Line inaugurated a twice-monthly service between Australia and Western Europe at freight rates substantially below those quoted by the Australia-to-Europe conference. At the same time, the Soviet line applied for admission to the conference and requested thirty-six sailings per year. The number of sailings sought was far in excess of Soviet trade with Australia and the conference denied the application. But the Soviets continued their service and by offering discounts of 15 to 20 percent from conference freight rates were able to obtain a number of contracts to carry Australian wool for European importers. In January, 1969, the Baltic Line was admitted to the conference, thus averting a potential rate war. Under the terms of the agreement the Soviets were permitted twelve northbound sailings and nine southbound sailings between Australia and Europe per year. Four of the northbound sailings largely serve ports in the USSR. The southbound sailings are from agreed continental and Baltic ports, including Finland. As a condition of membership, the Soviet line agreed to charge conference freight rates and to abide by other rules and conditions of the conference.[6]

Soviet shipping lines have employed rate-cutting tactics in a number of other instances, most recently in the transpacific trades between Japan and western North America. The Soviet Far East Shipping Line opened regular liner service between Japan and the west coast of Canada in December, 1968. This service was monthly at first, but became semimonthly in April, 1969, and in January, 1970, a third monthly voyage was reportedly added to U.S. ports in the Pacific Northwest. The Soviet liner rates are reported at about 15 percent below those quoted by the Trans-Pacific Freight Conference of Japan and the Japan–West Canada Freight Conference, which cover this route. The Soviet Far East Line was offered membership in these conferences, but as of January, 1970, it had not joined.[7]

Possible clues to interpreting Soviet shipping policy may be gained by reviewing the history of earlier Soviet excursions into the international economic arena; i.e., the commodity export programs launched by the USSR during the 1950's. The Soviet efforts to gain entry into the Australia-to-Europe Shipping Conference are in many

6. *Lloyd's List and Shipping Gazette* (London), February 18, 1969.
7. "USSR Making Steady Inroads in Shipping," *Shipping and Trade News* (Tokyo), January 1, 1970, pp. 3–4.

ways reminiscent of their earlier behavior in international commodity markets. Sudden increases in Soviet exports of staple commodities at reduced prices on a number of occasions resulted in sharp decreases in market prices and brought forth charges of Soviet dumping, and in some cases, of Soviet economic warfare against the Free World. Probably the greatest concern arose over Soviet petroleum exports, as illustrated by a study conducted by the National Petroleum Council of Soviet petroleum exports up to 1962, which concluded:[8]

> Thus, the communists are not out simply to sell oil, but among other things to disrupt, undermine and if possible, destroy the positions of the private oil industry. . . .
> The import of the Soviet attack on the private oil industry goes beyond its immediate implications to the companies involved. It is of great importance to the governments and peoples of the Free World. Reliance on an appreciable supply of Soviet oil provides the possibility of a strategic advantage to the communists in time of crisis when a sudden cut-off would require substantial efforts by the Free-World oil industry to restore normal lines of supply.

Later it became apparent that once the Soviets had established themselves in the market they modified their policies, and in general played by the established rules of the game, that is, they raised their prices to market levels and supported collusive agreements to restrict supplies and regulate prices.

The evolution of Soviet pricing policy with respect to petroleum exports is illustrated by the following statement from a Western petroleum industry publication:[9]

> In the 1950's and early '60's the Russians were determined to gain new outlets for their oil at almost any cost, and they were consequently prepared, in a good many cases, to underbid the established markets. In the last year or two, however, this policy has clearly been modified, at any rate in respect to the more highly developed regions. Not only have they held out for relatively high prices, notably in negotiations with Japan, but the chairman of Soyuznefteexport (the Soviet oil export organization) has himself attacked the main Western oil companies for allegedly selling oil at artificially low prices.

8. National Petroleum Council, *Impact of Oil Exports from the Soviet Bloc* (Washington: The Council, 1962), II, 443–44.

9. *Petroleum Press Service*, October, 1966, p. 366.

It thus developed that Soviet attempts to increase commodity exports through cut-rate pricing were not inspired so much by a desire to do injury to Western sellers as to earn badly needed hard-currency exchange. The Soviets were forced to sell at reduced prices as an "entrance fee" to world markets. In importing from the Soviet Union Western buyers frequently faced such disadvantages as poor credit facilities, inconvenient delivery schedules, and the lack of well-established distribution networks. To overcome these obstacles to trade the USSR was forced to offer its commodities at discount prices. Errors in judgment and inadequate Soviet knowledge of world-market conditions also contributed to low Soviet export prices.[10]

Soviet attempts to gain a larger share of world-shipping markets have led to fears of pernicious Soviet intentions similar to those that arose as a result of the earlier Soviet commodity export drives. For example, in November, 1968, at the time the Soviets were launching their foray against the Australia-to-Europe Shipping Conference, the press reported. "a gnawing fear among Western shipping sources that the Soviets will use their excess capacity to unleash a vicious rate war that would quickly drive privately owned ship operators to the wall."[11]

Such fears appear to be exaggerated. Soviet economic interests will probably lead to a much more benign shipping policy. The continued need for hard-currency exchange to finance imports from the West, and the limited opportunities available to the USSR for improving its hard-currency balances by alternative means, creates a strong incentive for the Soviets to maximize the earnings of these currencies by their merchant fleet. Such a policy would preclude the use of the merchant fleet as an instrument of economic warfare. Any political gains that the Soviets might achieve by this route likely would be short-lived and would risk the loss of foreign-exchange earnings because of adverse reactions of Western cargo owners. This is not meant to imply, however, that aggressive tactics of the type employed in the past will not be repeated whenever the managers of the Soviet merchant fleet calculate that it is in their short-term interest to do

10. Penelope H. Thunberg, "The Soviet Union in the World Economy," in *Dimensions of Soviet Economic Power,* Studies prepared for the Joint Economic Committee of the United States Congress (Washington: United States Government Printing Office, 1963), p. 440.

11. "Russia's Merchant Ships Ranging Afar, Peril West's Monopoly on Ocean Trade," *The Wall Street Journal,* November 18, 1968, p. 36.

so, but rather to suggest that Soviet shipping policy will be influenced more by the requirements of internal economic-development programs than by a desire to inflict economic or political injury on the West.

Notwithstanding the limitations on the ability of the Soviet merchant fleet to compete in world-shipping markets generally, and the forecast of a relatively cooperative shipping policy cited above, the USSR will continue to provide strong competition in a limited number of shipping trades. Analysis of comparative cost data shows that for the types of ships operated by the Soviet fleet their costs are not greatly in excess of those of other major merchant fleets. In addition, Soviet costs have declined as operations have expanded and the efficiency of their fleet has improved. For the reasons detailed in the preceding pages, however, Soviet competition in world shipping will remain limited in both scope and intensity. It follows that the Soviet fleet as it is presently constituted—and as it is projected for the next decade—does not seriously threaten to disrupt the world-shipping industry.

Appendix
Bibliography
Index

Appendix

TABLE A-1. *Capital Costs of Soviet Merchant Shipping, 1958–1965*

(millions of rubles)

	Capital Value of Transport Ships[a] (1)	Amortization Rate[b] (%) (2)	Capital Cost with Interest Rates of:			
			6% (3)	7% (4)	8% (5)	9% (6)
1958	757	1.01	54.8	62.4	70.0	77.5
1959	880	0.86	60.4	69.2	78.0	86.8
1960	1,004	0.94	69.6	79.7	89.7	99.8
1961	1,121	1.04	79.0	90.2	101.4	112.6
1962	1,267	1.04	89.2	101.9	114.6	127.2
1963	1,502	4.00	150.2	165.2	180.3	195.3
1964	1,624	4.00	162.4	178.7	194.9	211.2
1965	1,906	4.00	190.6	209.6	228.7	247.7
1966	2,146	4.00	214.0	235.4	256.8	278.2

a. See footnotes to Table 6.

b. L. S. Turetskiy and O. A. Novikov, *Amortizatsiya osnovnykh fondov morskogo transporta* (Moscow: Morskoy Transport, 1964), p. 32. Rates are for capital replacement.

TABLE A-2. Labor Costs in the Soviet Merchant Fleet, 1958–1965

	Number of Employees[a]	Average Annual Wage[b] (rubles)	Social Insurance Deduction[c] (rubles)	Berthing and Subsistence[c] (rubles)	Avg. Annual Labor Cost (rubles)	Total Annual Labor Cost (thous. rubles)
1958	44,500	1,175	79	294	1,548	68,886
1959	45,400	1,224	82	306	1,612	73,185
1960	47,900	1,272	85	318	1,675	80,232
1961	51,300	1,356	91	339	1,786	91,622
1962	53,700	1,440	96	360	1,896	101,815
1963	57,200	1,540	103	385	2,028	116,002
1964	63,300	1,579	106	395	2,080	131,664
1965	67,300	1,608	108	402	2,118	142,541

a. Tsentral'noye Statisticheskoye Upravleniye pri Sovete Ministrov SSSR, *Transport i svyaz' SSSR statisticheskii sbornik* (Moscow: Statistika, 1967), p. 159.

b. Tsentral'noye Statisticheskoye Upravleniye pri Sovete Ministrov SSSR, *Narodnoye khozyaistvo SSSR v 1965 g.* (Moscow: Statistika, 1966), p. 567. The wage data are for all water transport, 1959, 1961, and 1962 interpolated.

c. V. P. Kolomoytsev, *Cost of Maritime Shipping* (Washington: U.S. Department of Commerce, Joint Publications Research Service, Translation 14,874 p. 108. Social insurance deductions are set at 6.7 percent of basic wage fund; and berthing and subsistence charges run about 25 percent of money wages.

TABLE A-3. Expenditures in Foreign Voyages and Foreign-Exchange Expenditures by Soviet Ships

	Ton-km. All Voyages[a] (bil.)	Ton-km. Foreign Voyages[b] (bil.)	Cost/ Ton-km. All Voyages[c] (kop./10 ton-km.)	Cost of Shipments in Foreign Voyages as % of Cost of Shipments in All Voyages	Cost/ Ton-km. Foreign Voyages[e] (kop./10 ton-km.)	Expenditures in Foreign Voyages[f] (mil. rubles)	Foreign Exchange Expenditures[g] (mil. rubles)	Foreign Exchange Expenditures ÷ Expenditures in Foreign Voyages[h] (%)
1958	107.8	72.2	2.32	61	1.46	105.4	21.1	20.0
1960	133.3	94.6	2.12	67	1.42	134.3	23.0	17.1
1961	161.1	117.6	2.06	69	1.42	167.0	26.0	15.6
1962	175.4	131.5	2.00	71	1.42	186.7	26.6	14.1
1963	228.7	187.5	1.90	74	1.40	262.5	33.4	12.7
1964	300.4	246.3	1.67	74	1.24	305.4	35.1	11.5
1965	392.7	321.5	1.48	74	1.11	356.9	37.1	10.4
1966	444.5	364.4	1.46	74	1.08	393.6	37.0	9.4

a. Tsentral'noye Statisticheskoye Upravleniye pri Sovete Ministrov SSSR, *Transport i svyaz' SSSR statisticheskii sbornik* (Moscow: Statistika, 1964), p. 151; includes passenger traffic.

b. The percentages of total shipments accounted for by shipments in foreign voyages were: 67 in 1958; 71 in 1960; 73 in 1961; 75 in 1962; and 82 in 1963–66. The percentages for 1958 and 1963 are given in S. F. Koryakin and I. L. Bernshtein, *Ekonomika morskogo transporta* (2nd ed.; Moscow: Transport, 1964), p. 142; for 1960 and 1962 in V. A. Kolesnikov and Ye. D. Rodin, "Osnovnyye osobennosti morskogo transporta v sisteme yedinoy transportnoy seti SSSR," in *Ekonomika morskogo transporta morskoy transport v sisteme yedinoy transportnoy seti SSSR Trudy* 6(12) (Moscow: Transport, 1965), p. 12; 1961 and 1964–65 estimated.

c. *Transport i svyaz' SSSR*, p. 155.

d. S. F. Koryakin and I. L. Bernshtein, *Ekonomika morskogo transporta* (2nd ed., Moscow: Transport, 1964), p. 411 for 1958 and 1963, 1960–62 interpolated, 1964–65 estimated to be same as 1963.

e. Column 3 times column 4.

f. Column 2 times column 5.

g. See column 5, Table A-4, for 1958–63; 1964 and 1965 derived by multiplying column 6 by column 8.

h. 1958, 1960, 1961, and 1963 derived by dividing column 7 by column 6. Other years estimated by extrapolation of trend from 1958 to 1963.

TABLE A-4. *Foreign-Exchange Expenditures by Soviet Merchant Ships, Selected Years, 1957–1963*

	Expenditures per Billion Ton-Km. in Foreign Voyages (*thous. rubles*)[a]	Total Ton-Km. (*bil.*)[b]	% Foreign Voyages[c]	Ton-Km. Foreign Voyages	Foreign Exchange Expenditures (*mil. rubles*)
1957	362	94.1	65	61.2	22.2
1958	292	107.8	67	72.2	21.2
1959	267	117.2	69	80.9	21.6
1960	243	133.3	71	94.6	23.0
1961	221	161.1	73	117.6	26.0
1963	178	228.7	82	187.5	33.4

a. S. F. Koryakin and I. L. Bernshtein, *Ekonomika morskogo transporta* (2nd ed.; Moscow: Transport, 1964), p. 425 for 1957, 1959, 1961, and 1963; 1958 and 1960 estimated.

b. Tsentral'noye Statisticheskoye Upravleniye pri Sovete Ministrov SSSR, *Transport i svyaz' SSSR statisticheskii sbornik* (Moscow: Statistika, 1967), p. 59.

c. See footnote [b], Table A-3.

TABLE A-5. *Expenditures by the Soviet Merchant Fleet for Cargo Shipments in Foreign Voyages 1961–1965*

	Ton-Km. in Foreign Voyages[a] (*bil.*) (1)	Cost of Shipments Voyages[b] (*kopeks/10 ton-km.*) (2)	Cost of Shipments in Foreign Voyages as % of Cost of Shipments in All Voyages (3)	Cost of Shipments Foreign Voyages[c] (*kopeks/10 ton-km.*) (4)	Expenditures in Foreign Voyages[d] (*mil. rubles*) (5)
1961	116.1	1.87	69	1.29	149.8
1962	130.0	1.84	71	1.31	170.3
1963	185.6	1.74	74	1.29	239.4
1964	244.0	1.54	74	1.14	278.1
1965	318.7	1.38	74	1.02	325.1
1966	363.1	1.36	74	1.01	366.7

a. Tsentral'noye Statisticheskoye Upravleniye pri Sovete Ministrov SSSR, *Transport i svyaz' SSSR statisticheski sbornik* (Moscow: Statistika, 1967), p. 151. Freight only, passengers not included. See footnote [b] to Table A-3 for method of determining share of foreign voyages in total shipments.

b. *Ibid.*, p. 160.

c. Column 2 times column 3.

d. Column 1 times column 4.

TABLE A-6. *Expenditures and Income of Soviet Merchant Ships in Foreign Voyages, 1958, 1960, and 1964–1966*

(millions of rubles)

	Expenditures All Voyages[a]	Expenditures Foreign Voyages[b]	Foreign Voyages as % of Total[c]	Income All Voyages[d]	Income Foreign Voyages[e]
1958	246.3	105.4	42.8	261.5	111.9
1960	283.3	134.3	47.4	321.1	152.2
1964	503.1	305.4	60.7	607.1	380.6
1965	578.5	359.6	62.2	743.4	462.4
1966	651.1	393.6	60.5	861.2	521.0

a. Tsentral'noye Statisticheskoye Upravleniye pri Sovete Ministrov SSSR, *Transport i svyaz' SSSR statisticheskii sbornik* (Moscow: Statistika, 1967), p. 160.
b. Table A-3, column 6.
c. Column 1 times column 2.
d. *Transport i svyaz' SSSR* p. 160.
e. Column 3 times column 4.

TABLE A-7. *Estimated Geographic Distribution of Soviet Sea-Borne Foreign Trade, 1960 and 1964–1966*

(millions of rubles)

	% of Sea-Borne Trade in Total Foreign Trade[a]	1960 Total Trade[b]	1960 Sea-Borne Trade[c]	1964 Total Trade[b]	1964 Sea-Borne Trade[c]	1965 Total Trade[b]	1965 Sea-Borne Trade[c]	1966 Total Trade[b]	1966 Sea-Borne Trade[c]
Total foreign trade		10,073	4,886	13,878	5,895	14,610	6,918	15,079	7,378
Communist bloc									
East Europe	20	5,343	1,069	8,950	1,788	8,303	1,660	8,239	1,648
China	70	1,499	1,049	449	314	375	262	286	200
Other Asian area	70	146	102	246	172	256	179	245	172
Other	70	383	268	1,108	776	1,116	781	1,255	879
Other soft-currency areas	80	1,118	894	825	660	1,977	1,582	2,152	1,722
Hard-currency areas	95	1,584	1,504	2,300	2,185	2,583	2,454	2,902	2,755

a. Estimated on the basis of geographic location of countries concerned and commodity composition of trade with Soviet Union.
b. *Soviet Economic Performance 1966–67*, Material Prepared for the Joint Economic Committee, Congress of the United States (Washington: United States Government Printing Office, 1968), pp. 97–98 and 106. Converted to rubles at official rate, $1 = .9 rubles.
c. Column 1 times total trade.

TABLE A-8. *Soviet Imports of Ships and Marine Equipment*

(millions of rubles)

	1955[a]	1956[a]	1957[a]	1958[a]	1959[a]	1960[a]	1961[a]	1962[a]	1963[a]	1964[b]	1965[b]	1966[c]
Total	237.5	273.8	215.5	214.7	271.9	340.4	203.1	332.9	366.1	483.9	489.7	493.
Soft-currency countries	185.9	187.4	170.2	182.8	238.2	308.1	179.6	261.8	274.2	287.5	374.0	359.
Bulgaria	5.1	5.6	5.2	5.8	11.6	13.9	7.9	16.0	15.9	16.0	10.2	17.
Hungary	15.5	14.6	15.1	15.5	14.3	19.1	18.8	19.8	20.9	15.2	13.9	16.
East Germany	71.0	71.9	58.3	66.6	99.6	129.1	57.8	74.1	76.1	98.6	106.0	95.
Poland	28.1	24.4	29.0	35.5	42.5	56.1	36.3	59.9	71.4	84.3	94.6	96.
Rumania	11.3	12.9	10.5	7.3	8.9	10.9	7.5	8.7	12.3	12.3	14.1	11.
Czechoslovakia	10.1	12.1	13.8	15.2	14.2	19.9	19.1	16.9	19.6	23.9	23.0	25.
Finland	44.8	45.9	38.3	36.9	47.1	59.1	32.2	66.4	58.0	37.2	59.3	37.
Yugoslavia											52.9	59.
Hard-currency countries	48.3	86.4	45.3	31.9	33.7	32.3	25.5	71.1	91.9	196.4	115.7	133.
Britain		4.8	9.5	4.3	.3	.1	.1	.2	.6	.2	.4	7.
Denmark	5.7	4.5	1.5	.3	6.3	10.3	.2	10.7	16.6	15.0	17.1	14.
West Germany	14.7	30.1	7.9	18.4	1.7	5.9	4.1	16.1	23.8	34.3	24.1	38.
Netherlands	11.3	2.3	11.9	.1	.4	4.3	4.2	.2	.2	.9	13.9	8.
Sweden	7.5	12.3	.2	2.0	5.6	.2	1.8	1.8	.4	41.3	17.4	
Japan	.3	.6			7.3	10.5	3.5	33.8	31.4	61.6	34.9	53.
Italy				.1					9.1	29.1	7.6	
Other	12.1	31.8	14.3	6.7	12.1	1.0	13.8	8.3	9.8	14.0	.3	9.

a. Ministersvto Vneshnei Torgovli SSSR Planovo-Ekonomicheskoye Upravleniye, *Vneshyay torgovlya soyuza SSSR za 1959–1963 gody* (Moscow: Vneshtorgizdat, 1965), pp. 142–43.

b. *Vnesh. torg.*, 1965, p. 102.

c. *Vnesh. torg.*, 1966, p. 105.

TABLE A-9. Estimated Soviet Expenditures for Chartered Merchant Ships, 1961–1965

(millions of rubles)

	Tonnage Chartered (mil. tons)			Charter Rates ($ per ton)		Expenditures ($ mil.)		
	Total[a] (1)	Dry Cargo[b] (2)	Tanker[b] (3)	Dry Cargo[c] (4)	Tanker[d] (5)	Dry Cargo (6)	Tanker (7)	Total (8)
1961	19.3	9.7	9.6	5.84	4.38	56.6	42.0	98.6
1962	20.6	10.3	10.3	5.44	4.45	56.5	45.8	102.3
1963	19.0	9.5	9.5	6.15	5.27	58.4	50.1	108.5
1964	17.0	8.5	8.5	6.12	4.94	52.0	42.0	94.0
1965	13.3	6.6	7.7	6.15	4.77	40.6	31.3	71.9

a. Tsentral'noye Statisticheskoye Upravleniye pri Sovete Ministrov SSSR, *Transport i svyaz' SSSR statisticheskii sbornik* (Moscow: Statistika, 1967), p. 151.

b. Soviet sea-borne foreign-trade cargoes are divided about equally between dry-cargo and tanker tonnage; this is assumed to apply to charter cargoes as well.

c. Column 2, Table A-11.

d. See Column 3, Table A-12.

TABLE A-10. Estimated Rates Paid by the USSR for Chartered Dry-Cargo Vessels, 1965

Route[a] (1)	Rate[b] ($ per ton) (2)	Relative Weight[c] (3)	(2) × (3) (4)	Cargo (5)	Remarks (6)
Arctic–United Kingdom	8.80	.05	.440	lumber	1961 rates moved to 1965 by Soviet lumber index
Baltic–West Europe	3.91	.25	.977	coal and general	1963 and 1964 rates moved to 1965 by Soviet coal index
Black Sea–Med., Japan, and others	6.37	.40	2.548	general and pig iron	Weighted average of 1965 rates to Mediterranean, Japan, Persian Gulf, U.S., and West Africa
East Canada–Black Sea	8.20	.15	1.230	grain	1965 rates
Scandinavia–Baltic	3.00	.05	.150	general	Estimated on basis of Baltic –West Europe rate
South America–Black Sea	12.00	.05	.600	grain	1965 rates
Yugoslavia–Black Sea	4.20	.05	.210	general	Estimated on basis of Black Sea–Italy rate
Weighted average			6.155		

a. The seven routes shown account for the largest share, by far, of Soviet dry-cargo charters.

b. Maritime Research, Chartering Annual (New York, 1961–65), Vols. VII–XXII, except as noted in column 6. Most Soviet charters of dry-cargo vessels are single-voyage charters. Because of the difficulties in estimating the costs of time charters and consecutive voyage charters, single-voyage charter rates were applied to all charters.

c. Lloyd's List and Shipping Gazette (London, 1962–65). Estimates based on tonnage of chartered shipping listed for each route as percent of total for 1961–65 period; sample used consisted of first three months of 1961, second three months of 1962, third three months of 1963, fourth three months of 1964, and all of 1965.

TABLE A-11. *Estimated Rates Paid by the USSR for Chartered Dry-Cargo Ships, 1961–1965*

	Index of Charter Rates[a] (1965 = 100)	Rate Paid by USSR ($ per ton)
1961	95.0	5.84
1962	89.2	5.49
1963	100.0	6.15
1964	99.5	6.12
1965	100.0	6.15[b]

a. *Morskoy flot,* XXVI (November, 1966), pp. 18–19. The index of charter rates for dry cargoes is a composite of separate indexes calculated for voyage charters to carry the seven leading bulk cargoes in Soviet sea-borne foreign trade (lumber, fertilizers, grain, ore, coal, metals, and cement) between ports in the European regions of the USSR and foreign ports. The index is calculated on a 1960 base, but has been converted to a 1965 base for use here.

b. See Table A-10 for derivation on the average charter rate for 1965. The relative weights calculated for 1965 (Column 3 of Table A-10 are applied to the entire 1961–65 period).

TABLE A-12. Estimated Rates Paid by the USSR for
Chartered Tankers, 1961–1965

	Intascale[a] Rate for Soviet Charters[b] ($ per ton)	Index of Charter Rates[c] (Intascale — 100)	Rate Paid by USSR ($ per ton)
1961	6.20	70.7	4.38
1962	6.20	71.8	4.45
1963	6.20	85.0	5.27
1964	6.20	79.6	4.94
1965	6.20	77.0	4.77

a. Freight rates in the tanker market are generally determined as percentages of constant price scales. The index currently in use is the Intascale of the International Nominal Freight Association, Limited, which was adopted in 1962.

b. For the same reasons as those given for dry-cargo charters, single-voyage charter rates were applied to all charters (see footnote [b] to Table A-10). To simplify the calculations, the Intascale rates for the six primary routes for Soviet tanker charters were averaged. The weighting method used was the same as given for dry-cargo charters in footnote [c] to Table A-10. The average Intascale rate for these routes was calculated as follows:

	Rate ($ per ton)	Relative Weight	Col. 1 times col. 2 ($ per ton)
Black Sea to:			
India-Ceylon	5.00	.10	.500
Italy	2.28	.15	.342
Japan	9.59	.25	2.397
South America	6.92	.25	1.730
Scandinavia	4.77	.20	.954
West Africa	5.61	0.5	.281
Weighted average			6.204

c. *Morskoy flot*, XXVI (November, 1966), pp. 18–19. The index is expressed as a percentage of Intascale rates paid for all types of charters of Soviet and foreign tankers from Soviet and Rumanian ports on the Black Sea to all destinations. Separate indexes are calculated for "clean" and "dirty" vessels. The two indexes have been combined (with equal weights) for use here.

TABLE A-13. USSR: Outputs, Inputs, and Factor Productivity Trends in Industry, 1956–1965[a]

(1955 = 100)

	1956	1957	1958	1959	1960	1961	1962	1963	1964	1965
Index of output	109.4	119.5	131.2	144.6	155.8	168.1	181.8	194.4	207.6	222.7
Index of capital stock	112.0	124.1	138.1	153.7	171.5	191.7	212.2	236.5	262.2	287.8
Index of labor services	103.2	105.7	110.0	113.8	119.4	125.8	129.8	133.5	137.9	143.8
Index of factor inputs	105.7	116.6	117.3	123.8	132.2	141.6	149.0	156.7	165.1	174.7
Index of factor productivity	103.6	108.0	111.8	116.7	117.8	118.6	122.0	124.0	125.7	127.4
Index of labor productivity	106.0	113.1	119.2	127.0	130.5	133.7	140.1	145.6	150.7	154.9
Index of capital productivity	97.8	96.3	95.0	94.1	90.9	87.7	85.7	82.3	79.2	77.4

a. James H. Noren, "Soviet Industry Trends in Output, Inputs, and Factor Productivity," *New Directions in the Soviet Economy*, Studies Prepared for the Joint Economic Committee, Congress of the United States (Washington: United States Government Printing Office, 1966), Part II-A, Table 9, p. 316. Factor inputs based on employment data, 8 percent interest charges, and 1960 weights.

Bibliography

BOOKS

BAKAYEV, V. G. *Ekspluatasiya morskogo flota* (Operation of the Maritime Fleet). Moscow: Transport, 1965.

————. *SSSR na mirovykh morskykh putyakh* (The USSR on the World's Seaways). Moscow: Transport, 1969.

BERGSON, ABRAM, and SIMON KUZNETS (*eds.*). *Economic Trends in the Soviet Union.* Cambridge, Mass.: Harvard University Press, 1963.

FERGUSON, ALLEN R. *et al. The Economic Value of the United States Merchant Marine.* Evanston, Ill.: Northwestern University Press, 1961.

FISSER, FRANK M. *Tramp Shipping.* Bremen: Carl Schunemann Verlag, 1957.

GOLOVANOVO, A. L. *Transport SSSR* (Transport in the USSR). Moscow: Transport, 1967.

GRIPAIOS, HECTOR. *Tramp Shipping.* New York: Thomas Nelson & Sons, 1959.

KANTOROVICH, YA. B. *Ekonomika morskogo sudna* (Economics of the Maritime Ship). Moscow: Transport, 1964.

KLEIN, LAWRENCE R. *An Introduction to Econometrics.* Englewood Cliffs, N.J.: Prentice-Hall, 1962.

KOLOMOYTSEV, V. P. *The Cost of Maritime Shipping.* Washington: U.S. Department of Commerce, Joint Publications Research Service, Translation 14,874, 12 August 1962.

KORYAKIN, S. F., *and* I. L. BERNSHTEIN. *Ekonomika morskogo transporta* (Economics of Maritime Transport). 2nd ed.; Moscow: Transport, 1964.

139

MCKEAN, ROLAND N. *Efficiency in Government Through Systems Analysis.* New York: John Wiley & Sons, 1958.

MIKHAILOV, S. V. *Ekonomika mirovogo okeana* (Economics of the World's Oceans). Moscow: Ekonomika, 1966.

Ministerstvo Vneshnei Torgovlii SSSR Planovo-Ekonomicheskoye Upravleniye. *Vneshnyaya torgovlya soyuza SSR za 1959–1963 gody* (Foreign Trade of the USSR in 1959–1963). Moscow: Vneshtorgizdat, 1965.

Ministerstvo Vneshnei Torgovlii SSSR Planovo-Ekonomicheskoye Upravleniye. *Vneshnyaya torgovlya soyuza SSR za 1959 god* (Foreign Trade of the USSR in 1959). Moscow: Vneshtorgizdat, 1960.

————. *Vneshnyaya torgovlya soyuza SSR za 1965 god* (Foreign Trade of the USSR in 1965). Moscow: Mezhdunarodnyye Otnosheniya, 1966.

————. *Vneshnyaya torgovlya soyuza SSR za 1966 god* (Foreign Trade of the USSR in 1966). Moscow: Mezhdunarodnyye Otnosheniya, 1967.

MOORSTEEN, RICHARD. *Prices and Production of Machinery in the Soviet Union, 1928–1958.* Cambridge, Mass.: Harvard University Press, 1962.

National Bureau of Economic Research. *Output, Input, and Productivity Measurement.* Princeton, N.J.: Princeton University Press, 1961.

————. *The Theory and Empirical Analysis of Production.* New York: Columbia University Press, 1967.

O'LOUGHLIN, CARLEEN. *The Economics of Sea Transport.* London: Pergamon Press, 1967.

SHUKSTAL', YA. V., *et al. Transportnyye izderzhki v narodnom khozyaistve SSSR* (Transport Expenditures in the National Economy of the USSR). Moscow: Izdatel'stvo Akademii Nauk SSSR, 1959.

STURMEY, S. G. *British Shipping and World Competition.* London: The Athlone Press, 1962.

THORBURN, THOMAS. *Supply and Demand of Water Transport.* Stockholm: Business Research Institute, Stockholm School of Economics, 1960.

TISMER, JOHANNES F. *Die Schiffahrtpolitik und die Betriebsokonomie der Seeschiffahrt im Ostblock unter besonderer Berucksichtigung der Sowjetunion* (Merchant Shipping Policy and the Economics of Merchant Shipping in the East Bloc with Special Consideration to the Soviet Union). Berlin: Osteuropa-Institut, 1965.

TOPCHIY, S. M., T. F. SHULYANSKIY, *and* A. F. MIRONENKO. *Organizatisiya dvizheniya morskogo flota* (Organization of Traffic in the Maritime Fleet). Moscow: Morskoy Transport, 1962.

Tsentral'noye Statisticheskoye Upravleniye pri Sovete Ministrov SSSR. *Narodnoye Khozyaistvo SSSR v 1962 godu* (National Economy of the USSR in 1962). Moscow: Gosstatizdat, 1963.

Tsentral'noye Statisticheskoye Upravleniye pri Sovete Ministrov SSSR. *Narodnoye khozyaistvo SSSR v 1963 godu* (National Economy of the USSR in 1963). Moscow: Statistika, 1964.

―――. *Narodnoye khozyaistvo SSSR v 1964 godu* (National Economy of the USSR in 1964). Moscow: Statistika, 1965.

―――. *Narodnoye khozyaistvo SSSR v 1965 godu* (National Economy of the USSR in 1965). Moscow: Statistika, 1966.

―――. *Transport i svyaz' SSSR statisticheskii sbornik* (Transport and Communications in the USSR, a Statistical Compilation). Moscow: Statistika, 1967.

TURETSKIY, L. S., *and* O. A. NOVIKOV. *Amortizatsiya osnovnykh fondov morskogo flota* (Amortization of Fixed Capital in the Maritime Fleet). Moscow: Transport, 1963.

ULMER, MELVILLE, J. *Capital in Transportation and Public Utilities: Its Formation and Financing.* Princeton, N.J.: Princeton University Press, 1960.

ZAGLYADIMOV, D. P. *Razvitiye yedinoy transportnoy seti SSSR* (Development of a Unified Transport Network in the USSR). Moscow: Ekonomizdat, 1962.

REPORTS AND MONOGRAPHS

American Committee for Flags of Necessity. *The U.S. Controlled Bulk Carrier Fleet: A Study Presented to the President's Maritime Advisory Committee.* New York: May 5, 1965.

Central Intelligence Agency. *1955 Ruble-Dollar Price Ratios for Intermediate Products and Services in the USSR and the U.S.* Washington: The Agency, 1960.

―――. *1955 Ruble-Dollar Ratios for Construction.* Washington: The Agency, 1964.

―――. *A Comparison of Consumption in the USSR and the U.S.* Washington: The Agency, 1964.

Committee on Commerce, United States Senate. *The Soviet Drive for Maritime Power.* Washington: United States Government Printing Office, 1967.

―――. *The Growing Strength of the Soviet Merchant Fleet.* Washington: United States Government Printing Office, 1964.

Economic Report of the President. Washington: United States Government Printing Office, 1967.

KAPLAN, NORMAN M. *Soviet Transport and Communications: Output Indexes 1928–1962.* Santa Monica, Calif.: The Rand Corporation, 1964.

―――. *Soviet Transport and Communications: Output Indexes, 1928–1962.* Santa Monica, Calif: The Rand Corporation, 1965.

Maritime Research. *Chartering Annual*, VII (1961).

―――. *Chartering Annual*, VIII (1962).

―――. *Chartering Annual*, IX (1963).

―――. *Chartering Annual*, X (1964).

Maritime Research. *Chartering Annual,* XI (1965).
————. *Chartering Annual,* XII (1966).
National Petroleum Council. *Impact of Oil Exports from the Soviet Bloc.* Washington: The Council, 1964.
U.S. Department of Commerce, Maritime Administration. *The Soviet Merchant Marine.* Washington: United States Government Printing Office, 1967.

ARTICLES IN PERIODICALS

BAYEV, S. "Morskoy transport v chetvertii god semiletki" (Maritime Transport in the Fourth Year of the Seven-Year Plan), *Morskoy flot,* XXII (January, 1962), 1–3.
————. "Osnovnyye fondy morskogo transporta, ikh ispol'zovaniye, vosproizvodstvo platnost za nikh" (Fixed Capital in Maritime Transport, Its Utilization, Reproduction, and Payment For It), *Morskoy flot,* XXVII (February, 1967), 19–20.
FRUIT, RENÉ. "La Function de Production de Cobb-Douglas" (The Cobb-Douglas Production Function), *Revue Economique,* II (March, 1962), 186–236.
GOSS, R. O. "Investment in Shipping and the Balance of Payments: A Case Study of Import Substitution Policy," *Journal of Industrial Economics* XIII (March, 1965), 103–15.
HOOD, EDWIN M. (Interview). "An Interview with Edwin M. Hood," *Marine Engineering/Log,* LXXI, No. 2 (February, 1966), 48–51.
HUNTER, ALEX. "Some Notes on National Shipping Lines: The Australian Case," *The Economic Record,* XCIII (March, 1967), 20–46.
KAPLAN, NORMAN M. "The Growth of Output and Inputs in Soviet Transport and Communications," *The American Economic Review,* LVII (December, 1967), 1154–67.
KORSAKOV, E. "The System of Remuneration in the Soviet Merchant Marine," *International Labor Review,* XCIV (October, 1966), 398–414.
MCAULEY, ALASTAIR N. D. "Rationality and Central Planning," *Soviet Studies,* XVIII (January, 1967), 340–55.
"Novaya pyatiletka-zhivoye delo millionov" (The New Five-Year Plan—A Vital Concern of Millions), *Morskoy flot,* XXVI (April, 1966), 1–3.
PREST, A. R. *and* R. TURVEY. "Cost-Benefit Analysis: A Survey," *The Economic Journal,* LXXV (December, 1965), 683–735.
"Representative Market Quotations," *Petroleum Press Service,* XXXII (July, 1965), 156–58.
SELAND, JOHAN. "Shipping and the Balance of Payments," *Norwegian Shipping News,* XXIII (June, 1967), 57–66.
"Sovetskii frakhtovii indeks" (The Soviet Freight Index), *Morskoy flot,* XXVI (November, 1966), 18–19.

STURMEY, s. g. "National Shipping Policies," *Journal of Industrial Economics*, XIII (November, 1965), 14–29.

WILCZYNSKI, j. "Dumping and Central Planning," *Journal of Political Economy*, LXXIV (January, 1966), 250–64.

ARTICLES IN COLLECTION

BRONSON, DAVID W., *and* BARBARA S. SEVERIN. "Recent Trends in Consumption and Disposable Money Income in the USSR," in *New Directions in the Soviet Economy*. Studies Prepared for the Joint Economic Committee, Congress of the United States. Washington: United States Government Printing Office, 1966. Part II-B, pp. 495–530.

BUSH, KEITH. "Agricultural Reforms Since Khrushchev," in *New Directions in the Soviet Economy*. Studies Prepared for the Joint Economic Committee, Congress of the United States. Washington: United States Government Printing Office, 1966. Part II-B, pp. 451–72.

COHN, STANLEY H. "Soviet Growth Retardation: Trends in Resource Availability and Efficiency," in *New Directions in the Soviet Economy*. Studies Prepared for the Joint Economic Committee, Congress of the United States. Washington: United States Government Printing Office, 1966. Part II-A, pp. 99–132.

HEISS, HERTHA W. "The Soviet Union in the World Market," in *New Directions in the Soviet Economy*. Studies Prepared for the Joint Economic Committee, Congress of the United States. Washington: United States Government Printing Office, 1966. Part IV, pp. 917–33.

KOLESNIKOV, V. A. *and* YE. D. RODIN. "Osnovnyye osobennosti morskogo transporta v sisteme yedinoy transportnoy seti sssr" (Basic Peculiarities of Maritime Transport in the Unified Transport System of the USSR), in *Ekonomika morskogo transporta morskoy transport v sisteme yedinoy transportnoy seti SSSR Trudy 6 (12)*, Tsentral'nyy Nauchno-Issledovatel'skii Institut Morskogo Flota. Moscow: Transport, 1965. Pp. 5–12.

NOREN, JAMES H. "Soviet Industry Trends in Output, Inputs and Productivity," in *New Directions in the Soviet Economy*. Studies Prepared for the Joint Economic Committee, Congress of the United States. Washington: United States Government Printing Office, 1966. Part II-A, pp. 271–325.

POVALYAYEV, N. I. "Ekonomicheskiye pokazateli vos'mi i semichasovogo vakht i sudovykh rabot" (Economic Indexes for Seven-Hour and Eight-Hour Shifts in Shipboard Labor), in *Voprosy ekspluatatsiya morskogo transporta Trudy 7 (13)*, Tsentral'nyy Nauchno-Issledovatel'skii Institut Morskogo Flota. Moscow: Transport, 1965. Pp. 70–82.

REZ, R. S., *and* YU. I. BRZHEZHINSKII, "Puti sovershenstvovaniya organizatsii truda plavsostava" (Ways of Improving the Organization of Labor Aboard Ship), in *Ekonomika i ekspluatatsiya morskogo flota Trudy vypusk 70*, Tsentral'nyy Nauchno-Issledovatel'skii Institut Morskogo Flota. Moscow: Transport, 1966. Pp. 78–85.

RODIN, YE. D. "Voprosy rayonironvaniya i ratsionalizatsii morskikh soobshchenii" (Problems of Regionalization and Rationalization of Maritime Communications), in *Ekonomika morskogo transporta morskoy transport v sisteme yedinoy transportnoy seti SSSR, Trudy 6 (12)*, Tsentral'nyy Nauchno-Issledovatel'skii Institut Morskogo Flota. Moscow: Transport, 1965. Pp. 25–64.

THUNBERG, PENELOPE H. "The Soviet Union in the World Economy," in *Dimensions of Soviet Economic Power*. Studies Prepared for the Joint Economic Committee, Congress of the United States. Washington: United States Government Printing Office, 1962. Pp. 409–38.

NEWSPAPERS

Krasnaya zvezda (Red Star), March 13, 1966.
Lloyd's List and Shipping Gazette (London), 1962–65.
New York Times, The, October 13, 1969.
Shipping and Trade News (Tokyo), January 1, 1970.
Vodnyy transport (Water transport), April 26, 1966.
Vyshka (The Tower), February 19, 1969.
Wall Street Journal, The, November 18, 1968.

Index